Contents

Introduction	1
Materials, tools and methods of construction	5
The diary	15
Introduction to the diary	16
Sessions 1-17	17
Conclusion to the diary	71
Testing and care of your rod	73
Spliced rod joints – bamboo to go!	81
Some approaches to designing a rod	89
Epilogue	99
Sources of information and bibliography	102

Introduction

The pages that follow are concerned mainly with the making and use of a two-piece 8'0" split bamboo fly rod suitable for river fishing for trout, grayling or any other fish that feels inclined to take a floating dry fly, emerger pattern, or sunk nymph and they are part of a process that started more than forty years ago when my interest was first drawn to making such rods. There are also some 'supporting' sections on materials, methods of construction, rod design, use and care of the rod, etc. I debated whether or not to include these items as many other books offer such information and initially my intention was to simply set down the diary, but when that was done the project seemed somehow incomplete so the extra chapters found a place. As the writing proceeded it seemed to develop a life of its own, so that processes and ideas that might not be regarded as 'main stream' thoughts found their way on to the pages. Again after some consideration it was decided to let these entries stand as well since much (maybe most) of the enjoyment of the subject throughout the years has come from experimenting with and developing, albeit small, personal ideas and processes, most of which appear in the notes that accompany the diary entries. Readers will also find some references to bow making along with a few illustrations as this is another craft that has captivated me for rather longer than rod making. When I think of one activity I tend also to think of the other as they both lead to the production of objects that are used in very dynamic, even dramatic, ways and have much in common in historical development, use of materials, practical techniques and conceptual considerations and, perhaps more importantly, because both are excellent fun, which I hope is what this booklet is really about.

My conversion to bow making was 'Pauline' and occurred the moment I found a copy of *The Archers' Craft* by A. J. Hodkin on the oversized book section of the local library when I was 15 years old and thus some years beyond the hedgerow stick phase of bow making that afflicts (or did afflict) somewhat younger boys. I was not exactly struck from my horse but I knew straightaway, without doubt, that I wanted to make a 'proper' bow. Rod making however stole up on me more secretly about a decade later and had its foundation in my delight in fishing from as far back as I can remember – memories of minnows and sticklebacks captured in bread baited jam jars, of smelt when on holiday by the seaside and of the grander sorts that came later, beautiful roach and worm hungry perch to name just two, and of course the game fish that are the principal quarry of split bamboo fly rods. (I still enjoy catching minnows with a size 24 hook and a matchstick float but I tend not to advertise the fact too widely.)

The first proper bow was made fifty years ago (to the year as I write) and the first split cane rod followed about a decade later, so I was a bowyer before a rod maker and a fisherman before both, though in the early days these claims certainly described my expertise in a fairly loose sense. The main thing however is that I am still at all three on a very regular basis, still enjoy them greatly and like to think that my skill at all three has improved by quite some measure. The idea of sustaining an interest over a long period of time is something that I believe has a very enriching sort of value that goes beyond the simple accumulation of knowledge of the particular activity, and although I would not wish to have to define what I mean I am sure it is very beneficial for those who have the inclination and are able to 'stay the course' even when things get a bit difficult, as they are sure to do sometimes.

When the notion of making a split bamboo rod first entered my head it was dismissed as being beyond me: the whole business looked so complicated and seemed to be enveloped in more than its fair share of mystery and the amount of informative literature and advice and access to it was much more limited than it is today. Some ideas however have a sly capacity for anchoring themselves and of working away inside one's head, establishing themselves initially as possibilities, then probabilities and finally as things that must be attempted whether success or failure is to be the outcome. Despite these misgivings there were some encouraging aspects to the idea: like bow making, it is what I term a small-scale enterprise which does not require large amounts of workshop space and materiel and allows the amateur to substitute hand skills and techniques for work that would otherwise have to be done with quite complicated and expensive machinery and yet still allows him to produce items of the highest quality (dare I say as good or even better than some manufactured products?) when some thought and effort have been expended and experience gained.

For those in the amateur setting who feel inclined to make a rod even today it will not be a wholly undemanding enterprise and the more initial skill, craft experience, imagination and equipment that can be brought to bear at the outset the greater will be the chances of initial success. However the longer I spend at this type of work the more convinced I become that the very best attribute a person can apply to the project is a 'fixed' desire to make a rod or a bow or whatever. Such an attitude will almost certainly ensure that some level of success is achieved provided that participants do not hem themselves in with tight schedules and unrealistic initial expectations and are willing to travel over the bumpy bits as readily as the smooth, and it may well be a journey that is quicker, more enjoyable and fruitful if a travelling companion can be found, which in my case was unfortunately not possible. The Internet now allows those who might feel isolated to gain knowledge and share ideas in a manner that was pretty well inconceivable not very long ago – it is a mine of information.

Despite the last paragraph this booklet is not intended primarily as a DIY manual, rather it is a record of a few decades of rod making expressed through the diary and the pieces that accompany it – though the impulse to encourage those readers who have not made a rod to do so will surely become all too apparent in places. There is always something to be learned even when someone has been involved in the pursuit for ages and if the Internet or contact with a rod maker is not available then seeking out books and other publications is the way to proceed. I would urge readers to search out as much information as possible and sift through it so that as informed a choice as possible can be made about how to proceed or simply to become better informed and to test what is written in the pages that follow. This, after all, is just one person's opinion of how the craft may be approached, which over the years has led to the making of about seventy rods. Such a number is certainly not large when compared with say the output of those who have made a living from rod making, but I suspect it is quite a respectable amount for the amateur setting where solutions to the questions posed have had to be answered within that setting.

Before finishing this introduction I wish to say that the word 'amateur' in this booklet is used simply to differentiate between those who make rods as a hobby and those who do so on a commercial basis and it has nothing at all to do with the modern (and incorrect) use of the word which describes something that is shoddy or second rate.

I hope that you enjoy and find informative what follows, that it will cause at least a little debate and maybe even encourage some to make a rod.

Materials, tools and methods of construction

The pages of this chapter describe briefly the materials and methods of construction that I have used to make rods for various types of fishing but predominantly for fly fishing over the years and indicate that there are a number of ways in which a rod may be made. As time has passed the solutions to the problems have evolved and changed as experience has been gained so some of the methods initially described below have been superseded by those that appear later. No claims are being made that what follows is in any sense a definitive statement about how a rod should be made as many other amateur rod makers will have developed other ways of proceeding that are just as valid as what is written below.

Materials and tools

The bamboo that interests built cane rod makers today is Tonkin cane that comes from southern China and is identified from the hundreds of other types by the Latin name *Arundinaria amabilis* meaning the Lovely Bamboo, a description that rod makers will not disagree with particularly when they lay their hands on a really fine, blemish free culm (the correct term for a pole) with a large diameter, thick walls and fine, neatly formed nodes. This type of bamboo is also known in China as Tea Stick Bamboo among other things though quite why this is so you will have to ask the Chinese. In the past rods have been made from other sorts of cane including one called Calcutta cane and a type grown in Japan but in the main these have been set aside in favour of Tonkin. The only other sorts of bamboo I have any experience of are the ornamental ones that grow in the garden, those used for bean sticks and a huge type from which material can be cut for making, among other things, landing net frames and archery bows in addition to the structural horticultural features that are the usual use of such poles.

Rod makers' Tonkin is normally available to the amateur in various lengths up to six feet if it is delivered or twelve if it is collected from the suppliers. The outside diameter will vary from say 1½" to about 2½" as will the wall thickness from about ³⁄₁₆" to ⁵⁄₁₆" or more depending on which part of the culm it is taken from, the thicker more robust sizes coming from the butt and the finer ones from the top end. Such wall dimensions will allow the triangular strips that will make up the rod section to be made wholly from the primary or power fibres which are those closest to the outside surface of the pole, the inside ones being too soft for rod making purposes. Indeed as few of these outside fibres as possible should be removed during the building process so their remarkable properties can be transferred from the parent pole to the rod; properties of strength, stiffness, and vitality that made split bamboo rods 'the' rods to own in the past and even today command the attention and interest of some anglers in this age of marvellous synthetic alternatives. The number of nodes to be found in a 6'0" pole will vary with an average pole, if one can claim that there is such a thing, having about six which are likely to be slightly closer together at the thicker end, though some poles may have as few as four. The roundness and general quality can vary, with the very best being beautifully circular and of very 'even' appearance with very straight grain which when split does so in a straight line down the whole length of the pole and not in a zig-zag fashion and/or a (gentle) spiral.

The colour of a pole can vary but ideally it should be a light buff brown, though sometimes I have received a pole with a very slight greenish hue which initially caused me a bit of consternation as most books say that such poles should be avoided. In practice however once they have been kept in a warm place for a while and heat treated during the rod making process they produce rods that are indistinguishable in both appearance and performance from those made from buff poles. I would however much prefer not to have one of these deviants as I feel that I should get rid of the green – or is this unnecessary and am I wasting my time – will the fish know? I have speculated whether such poles have been treated differently from the normal ones which are subjected to quite a lengthy seasoning in the hot sun of southern China amongst other things before being heated over a crucible of hot coals which allows any marked naturally occurring bends to be removed in much the same way as the bends are removed from blank sections before they are converted into a rod. A shortening of the seasoning in the sun or the elimination of the straightening process may well account for the greenish colour; Tonkin bamboo as it grows is quite a dark green if the photographs I have seen are true images of the plant.

The cost at the time of writing of about £10–20 for a 6'0" pole seems modest enough given that it has travelled halfway around the world and from which a rod with two tops can be made that may last for decades. Thus cost of the actual raw material is not really an issue for the amateur, though the accessories – rod rings, ferrules, reel seats and particularly corks, depending on their quality – can be surprisingly expensive when compared with the cost of the pole.

Many things will happen to a pole when it is made into a rod by hand – it will be split, straightened, planed, tempered, glued, etc. The strips of bamboo have to be made in formers of one sort or another that are made from either wood or metal. My first attempts to make a rod involved the use of triangular formers made from mahogany which were superseded by grooved boards made from beech wood which in turn gave way to an adjustable type made from mild steel – all materials that are readily available. The strips of bamboo created in these formers have to be glued together which I have done principally with Cascamite One Shot, an excellent, simple to use and durable adhesive which does the job excellently though reference will be found in the pages to come of a number of other sorts of glue that I have also used. Protecting the rod from the elements requires the application of a few coats of appropriate top quality 'finish' such as polyurethane, spar varnish or two part cellulose type.

The tools that are required fall into two categories, the first of which is likely to be found in the workshop of the averagely equipped general craftsperson and the second that will not as it is rod making specific; it is this second group that is likely to test the ingenuity of those starting in the craft unless they wish to spend significant amounts of money purchasing custom-made items that are now available. The specialised items of equipment can be made in the workshop which can prove an interest (or a trial!) in itself but by doing so a good depth of understanding will be developed about the craft. It is inevitable, when one has been at something for decades, that much collecting together of appropriate stuff will have occurred, as will become apparent as the pages of the diary are read. However in my case this accumulation occurred gradually and it is true to say that the first few dozen rods were made with a much more basic kit of equipment than has been available latterly. As the diary is read the tools and equipment referred to here will be expanded on as the various processes are set out, some of which might surprise with their simplicity as I have a great liking for the idea of achieving a particular end in as simple a fashion as possible commensurate with the production of a high class item. I have heard tell of rods being made literally on the kitchen table although this seems a bit extreme even to a lover of the uncomplicated; I am sure, for example, that a workshop, even one of very modest size, is a fairly indispensable facility if household harmony is to be maintained.

Methods of construction

Most modern split bamboo fly rods are of hexagonal cross section and are made from six strips of material that are glued together to form a rod's section though some makers specialise in producing rods of different cross-sectional shapes. For example, pentagonal and four-sided (quadrant) rods have their adherents but I suspect their number comprises only a small percentage of those who make the six-sided type, possibly because they cannot be fabricated with the simplicity of their hexagonal counterparts. A regular hexagon can be built up from six equilaterally triangular sectioned strips in which all the angles are 60° and all the sides the same length, a facility that the pentagon and the square do not afford. In practical usage there seems to be no measurable advantage in using one regular polygonal cross-sectional shape over another so the choice of one that can most easily be made up is a sensible one. This is not strictly true (whatever is?) as the stress created in sections with odd numbers (for example the pentagon) is greater than in those with even numbers given that the rod rings have to be mounted on a 'flat' which means that the apex opposite this flat will be farther away from the neutral axis of the polygon and thus subject to measurably more stress than the opposite face. Quadrant rods do not suffer from this inequality of stress but, given that they too have to be made from a round culm, they may require rather too great a proportion of the power fibres to be removed if a flat-sided section is to be produced. If one wishes to make rods with a number of sides other than six then it would seem sensible to choose a larger, even numbered/regular polygon, say eight, which creates a section that is not subject to the uneven stress inherent in one of uneven number and will require the removal of less of the bamboo's power fibres to create a flat-sided shape to which the guides can be attached.

I have experimented with flat strip bamboo construction that has led to complete rods of round cross section being made and top sections for rods that have otherwise been constructed of other woods such as ash and greenheart. Such rods however have been at the margins of my rod making though their building and use was very interesting and has allowed some old rods to be rejuvenated, for some working facsimiles to be made and for a greenheart rod that I bust on the East Lyn river on Exmoor to be successfully repaired thirty years later – which is still given a short airing at some point each season.

The 60° (equilaterally sectioned) strips of bamboo that go to make up a hexagonal rod section lie at the heart of built cane rod making. If these triangular strips (or splines as they are referred to) are properly made in respect of both their sectional accuracy and their taper then there is every chance that a good rod will result; they are the core element in making a split bamboo rod and I would have to be presented with a very compelling argument to make me alter this opinion. Of course all the other rod making tasks have to be done competently but these are not so hard to master as producing top quality splines (and the boards in which to make them). I am sure that anyone who has got as far as making good splines is going to have little difficulty in coping with the remaining processes.

The photograph here shows a selection of formers/boards that have been used at various times over the past forty years to produce splines. These can be regarded as a chronological statement of my attempts to produce rods of increasing quality, an objective that has been largely achieved, though the use of the adjustable metal and wooden boards did not so much improve their quality but rather speeded up their production and added greatly to the convenience with which rods of differing tapers could be produced, i.e. they allow one to be very versatile in respect of spline size.

The equilaterally triangular cross-sectioned former shown is made from hardwood, mahogany in this case, and is rather longer than the rod section that is to be produced on it – about 6″ longer. It has its apexes planed away along its whole length, the amount of material removed being precisely the same as the splines required for the rod. On to each 'flat' a piece of 'overhanging' bamboo is glued and when these overhangs are planed off the former's original shape is reconstituted; the bamboo is then removed and the process repeated until one has enough to make a rod section. All this is perfectly easy to set down on paper but in reality it was the perfect epitome of Sod's Law for me, a law which says that 'a piece of bread and butter dropped on the floor always lands butter side down'. In this situation it manifested itself differently but no less perversely as rarely could I get the bamboo strip to stick properly to the small flat surface – it would stick in some areas but not in others or it would pop off at some critical moment, etc. When perseverance enabled me to get it glued on and planed I could then never get the blasted thing off without mutilating the bamboo, the former and my temper, the latter to a considerable degree. I did

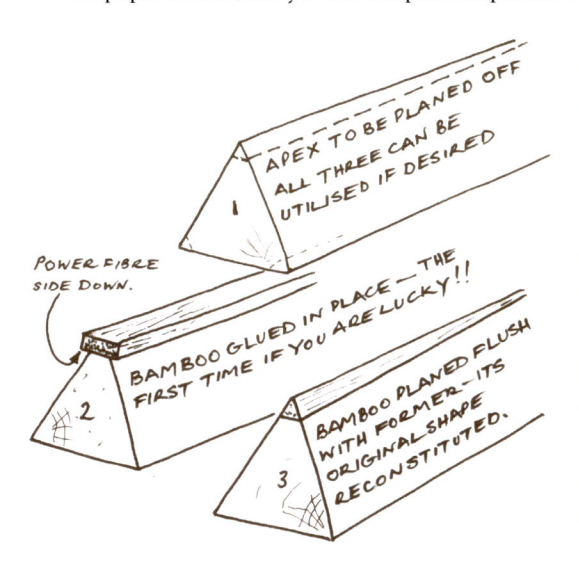

A triangular salmon rod former has been kept purely for demonstration purposes

use this method to make a replacement centre for a coarse fishing rod right at the start of my rod making escapades which was coarse not only in name though it did play its part in landing an 8lb carp but I think that that said more for the exceptional qualities of Tonkin bamboo than the quality of the rod section which I immediately retired from active service. It did not take me long to decide that some other way of making splines would have to be found if I was to continue with the activity. I do take my hat off to those who habitually make their rods in this manner, but fortunately for me it was not a case of TINA (there is no alternative) – which I guess is rarely so.

The second method employed involved substantial wooden boards with 60° grooves cut in them in which the bamboo could be planed. These boards can be made from a variety of timbers: mine, for convenience, were/are made from beech, an easy- to- work, stable and cheap indigenous wood. Typically a board will be say 3" or 4" wide by 2" deep and rather longer than the rod sections that are to be made in it; it needs to be trued up either by hand or on a mechanical planer and then have the grooves cut in it. Some of the grooves will be parallel sided (constant depth) and others will be tapered (varying depth) and in the days before hand held mechanical routers became a common workshop tool cutting these posed a problem until the device shown in the photograph below was made.

Paper build up visible under metal runners

The 60° HHS cutter is held in its retaining block at 90° to the surface of the board and can be adjusted for depth of cut and lateral movement across the board. Parallel grooves are quite easily made but the tapered ones require some effective means of controlling the varying depth of cut. Initially these tapered grooves were made by altering the setting (depth) of the cutter at intervals (3" or 6") along a board's length which made grooves that led to perfectly satisfactory rods, despite the fact that they were in reality a series of steps. This was a tedious business both in terms of having to constantly reset the depth of cut and because one wrong setting would upset all the subsequent ones. However when I happened on the idea of screwing tapered runners temporarily to the edges of a board's 'working' surface along which the cutter could be moved the whole business of groove cutting specifically and rod making in general took another step forward. The 'slope' or taper of the runners was controlled by packing their undersides with strips of paper. Now this may seem a really Heath Robinson way of proceeding and I suppose it is, but it has the advantage of working beautifully as good quality paper is made to very fine tolerances

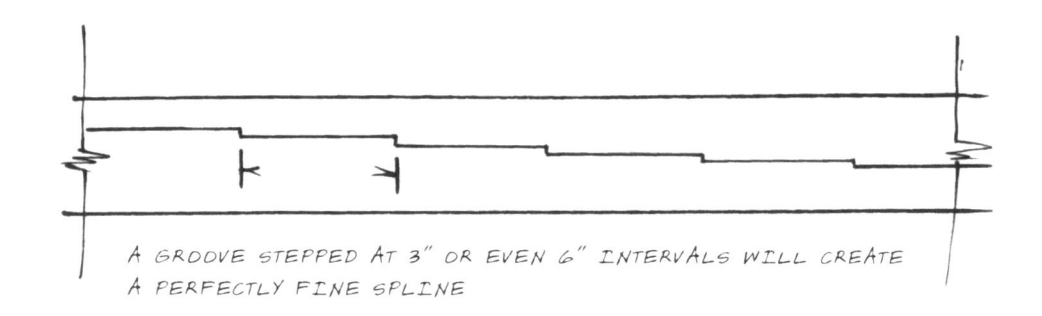

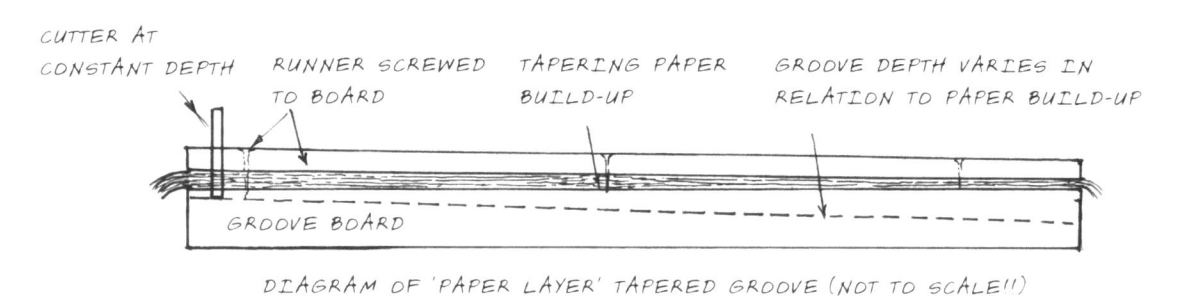

A GROOVE STEPPED AT 3" OR EVEN 6" INTERVALS WILL CREATE A PERFECTLY FINE SPLINE

DIAGRAM OF 'PAPER LAYER' TAPERED GROOVE (NOT TO SCALE!!)

hardly varying in thickness (maybe ½ a thou over its whole spread) so accurate build-ups are possible. As the cutter, set at a certain depth, is moved along the board where the build-up is thick the groove will be shallow with the converse being the case where it is thin. At one time I used to search out paper of different thicknesses to create the tapers but later set that method aside in favour using paper of constant thickness (4 thou) and altering the spacings between the layers (of paper) which of course also altered the degree of taper at the required points along the board/groove.

A typical 'set' of boards will comprise one with a number of parallel grooves of differing depths, another with a selection of tapered grooves and finally a board with two tapered grooves, one for the tip and the other for the butt (for a two-piece rod), which are cut precisely to the size of spline required for a particular rod. This final board has to be very carefully made but once made removes all the problems and anxious moments wondering whether the final splines are the correct size or not. I have a number of 'final size' boards in which dozens of rods have been made over the years and are still in use today. An alternative way of producing the final sized splines is to make a series of grooved boards in the manner just described with different constant tapers in which the splines can be successively planed. For example, a selection of grooves that taper 4, 5, 6, 7, 8, 9 thou, etc. per 5", some of suitable depth for top sections and others for butts, can be cut in boards say 60" long. The splines can then be planed in the appropriate sequence of grooves to produce the required compound taper and obviously the greater the variety of tapers that are cut the more versatile you can be. When the diameters of many rods are measured it will often be found that sections of them are made up of different constant tapers which can then be produced in this type of board. Such boards are not so difficult to make as the 'final' sized ones described but of course the sequential planing requires more thought so there are benefits and disadvantages with both methods.

The steel boards shown in the photograph are the latest development, one that further speeded up the whole business of making a rod with new tapers. They were made in the workshop at home, the one that seems to be constantly overflowing with 'stuff' however hard I try to reduce the general chaos. How they work is not difficult to understand though they did take quite some time and physical effort to make with very limited engineering equipment where hand work had to be substituted for power tools. I comforted myself with the thought that all the exercise would make me strong enough to heft the largest cane rod all day without fatigue – the draw-filing in particular made my arms ache – but what is it that is said? 'No gain without pain' or some such rubbish! Well, before the task was finished I would happily have let someone else have all the pain if I could have contrived to have the gain, but who wouldn't? Maybe it was stubbornness or more likely stupidity that saw the job finished; in such situations a bit of bloody-mindedness can be very useful as it is something that ordinary people can employ as a partial substitute for natural talent. Instant and easy success is the preserve of the innately gifted, the lucky blighters. (Don't you just hate them – you shouldn't of course but privately it is rather delicious to do, don't you think?) Over time however, even for ordinary mortals, the level of one's worst performance will improve which I suppose is one way of measuring increasing skill.

ONE GROOVE IS LARGER THAN THE OTHER BY A FEW THOU BUT THE TAPER IS THE SAME

A 'board' can be made from two bars of bright drawn mild steel 20mm x 20mm x 1730mm (0.75" x 0.75" x 68") that are joined together and have a 60° vee groove cut symmetrically down the long axis. The bars are squared off by draw-filing before having holes drilled and tapped in them at intervals, usually 5", along their length for bolts that allow them to be opened or closed and for location pins that hold the two halves in the correct relationship to one another. One half of the vee is created on an edge of one bar and the other half, its mirror image, is cut on the appropriate edge of the second bar.

Drilling *Tapping*

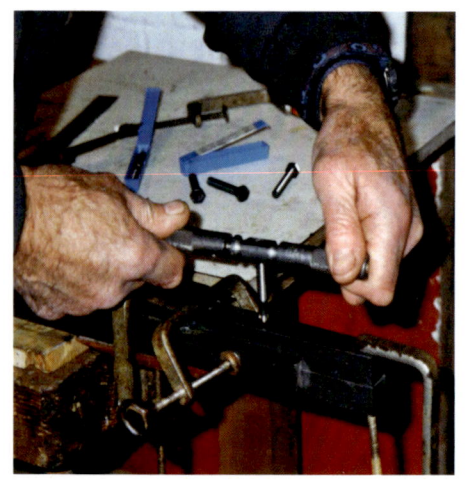

12 | **Materials, tools and methods of construction** | The diary of a rod

The correct angle is initially formed by holding the bars, each in turn, in a 60° jig and draw-filing the protruding corner level with the top of the jig, the required taper again being formed with paper build-ups placed under the bar. It goes without saying that the jig must be made and used in as accurate a fashion as possible, however it is usually the case that the groove will benefit from being dressed finally with a 60° triangular file glued to a small block of wood so that when the two halves of a board are fully closed they form a precise 60° angle. The taper along the length of the vee groove must be constant (straight) which ensures that it will produce straight-sided tapering splines with no unwanted 'widenings' or 'narrowings'. Provided these important points are achieved the exact taper and depth of grooves are not (within certain narrow limits) of vital importance as the width of the grooves will be adjusted with the set bolts, one proviso being that the vee, when fully closed, must not be larger than the strip of cane to be formed in it as it is clearly not possible to make an accurate spline if it fits loosely in the groove. A typical taper will be say 1 thou per inch and a typical groove for a top section of a rod when fully closed will taper in depth from 20 thou" to 80 thou" over 60", which is a useful board length, however a taper of say 30 to 90 thou" would be quite acceptable provided that rods with very fine tips will not be required. A board for butt sections will taper from say 70 thou" to 130 thou" over 60" which means that the sizes at the thick end of the smaller groove overlap those of the larger which is a great help particularly when three-piece rods are being made.

60° jig holding bar

The steel boards I have made have two grooves each in them, one on each side, that have the same taper but differ in depth by a few thou when fully closed which allows for the making of a wide range of rods; one board has grooves for butt sections and the other has grooves for tip sections. These are used in conjunction with the wooden preparation boards described above which reduce the wear to which the more difficult to make steel boards would otherwise be subjected. If a rod with some special feature such as a swelled butt is required then the swell will be made in a short adjustable wooden board that has been made specifically to produce that feature. Indeed adjustable wooden boards of the same design as steel ones can be made either with metal bushings to accept the adjustment bolts or simply with the threads cut directly into the wood which is the method I used to make the swelled butt board. As I do not greatly favour rods with extremely swelled butts and very

Dressing tools

rarely make them I proceed in this fashion rather than use the adjustment bolts to force one of my standard steel boards excessively or enlarge it permanently with a file so that it becomes useless when smaller sized butts are subsequently required. Of course one could make a separate adjustable steel board with a swell.

Only one of the items just described was made outside my averagely equipped workshop and that was the 60° groove cutter for wooden boards, part of which was made on a metal milling machine in a school workshop. The only 'special' tools necessary for making the steel boards were taps, reamers and a small pillar drill, if you can refer to a drill costing less than £40 special – there were more thought and effort than money involved.

Today a would-be rod maker is able to equip himself with custom-made equipment with which to make his rods and thus save himself the bother of trying to produce it himself which has been touched on above. However I am not sorry that things were different in the past and demanded the application of quite a bit of thought and ingenuity if rods of decent quality and the tools with which to make them were to be obtained. Such input was accepted as 'part of the process'; in many ways it was comparable to serving a sort of self taught apprenticeship. Maybe also this inevitably rather more drawn out approach left the rod maker with a greater understanding of the many aspects of the craft that otherwise might have passed him by.

Two rods 6'0" and 7'0" respectively made 30 years apart in the same 'final size' groove boards

The diary

Introduction to the diary

The diary that follows is divided into the work sessions that took place to bring 'The Diary Rod' into being. Each session has a section of 'Notes' which, amongst other things, expand on the details already recorded in the work sessions, record alternative ways of proceeding that have been adopted at different times and in some instances include suggestions and ideas that might be regarded as speculative. In the main everything that is included in the notes has at some point or other been tried or experimented with as the years have passed though not all are now part of my 'standard' procedure.

I have decided that this account will not be sanitised in any fashion but will record the mishaps as well as the 'triumphs' (which I am quite as prone to claim as the next man!) which I hope might act as an encouragement to those who may be a little hesitant about trying to make a rod and also not leave the impression that everything was learned and carried out with a sort of languid ease.

The work sessions were not all of the same duration nor did they take place on consecutive days but were spread over a period of a couple of months as there was no great hurry to get the project completed and at times the workshop was rather too cold a place to be; January and February are not the best months for rod making in my workshop (or maybe I am just getting softer as the years go by).

Each session was timed to produce an accurate record of how long it took to build the rod in a manner that is as 'hand built' as you are likely to encounter in the hope that it might encourage those who have just thought about making a rod to do so.

Now it is time to do some rod making.

A photograph like this encourages the rod making progress

Session 1

Whether today's work should be called a 'session' or not is open to question as all that was done was to gather together the various things that would be required, prepare the tools and buy a couple of items, however as a diary has to start somewhere this seemed as good a place as any.

Normally there is no difficulty in doing the above but recently the workshop was moved to a new location and the rod making gear was stored away in various places. As a consequence of this I had to play hide and seek with the spare block plane blades for ages. This put me in mind of a similar game played with the children when they were small and we were on holiday which went on far too long for the peace of mind of the parents and ended like this.

Father Didn't you hear us calling you?

Child Yes.

Father Why didn't you answer then?

Child You said to be very quiet and stay hided.

All of which was true and to which there was no adequate riposte so we all went off and had an ice cream. I wished however on many occasions after that such obedience had always been the norm! The spare blades, when found, did not get off so lightly and were reprimanded in language quite unsuitable for young ears and given a sharpening that was rather brisker than necessary by way of a reminder not to be so difficult in the future, based on the belief that such objects are not so inanimate as they would have us believe.

A good looking pole 6'0" long and rather more than 2" in diameter that had already been split in half was chosen from a small store, some of which have been 'waiting' their turn for more than 20 years. It was selected after being weighed in the hand, looked at and generally pondered upon – not a very precise way of proceeding but one that seems perfectly adequate in separating the good from the mediocre; not all things to do with rod making proceed in a strictly technical and scientific way I am pleased to say.

The purchase of some fresh glue and a few cards of strong linen thread completed the gathering together of what I needed.

Whose turn is it this time? Some of the poles in the woodstore, others are stored all about the place in the warm and dry which they like rather as we do.

Making a choice which is done by intuition rather than anything else – feel, colour, weight, wall thickness all come into this not very definable practice.

Notes

Tools and formers

Many of the tools that are required are of the general sort that are to be found in the workshop of an adequately equipped woodworker of some experience, ordinary things like a jack plane, block plane, clamps, rasps, files, etc., a bench to work on with a vice to secure things and of course at least some of the rod making items mentioned in the previous chapter.

Some publications that are in most respects quite excellent can sometimes leave the impression that a great host of tools are a prerequisite for making a rod – something that I do not believe to be the case. Take for example a scraper plane which is a tool that it would be very nice to have but is in no way essential for making a rod, because a hand cabinet scraper traditionally made from a piece of hand saw blade or in the form of a type of large spoke shave or even a piece of abrasive paper wrapped around a cork block will act as perfectly adequate alternatives until such a plane is obtained if ever it is. As you read the succeeding pages you will see that there are numerous simple solutions to the problems that arise and, as time passes, you will certainly develop your own ideas and gadgets in this respect.

The larger sort of bamboo produces a coarser grained material than rod building Tonkin that is nevertheless excellent for archery bow cores

I suppose that what I am really trying to do here is to encourage those who have only the faintest impulse to make and use their own rod not to be put off at the outset by the thought that not having a huge range of gear instantly available automatically rules out any chance of success – nothing need be farther from the truth as many people commence in a modest sort of way and build up their resources and expertise over time which has an interest factor all its own quite irrespective of the craft that is being undertaken. One item that you cannot do without however is a micrometer.

AN ITEM THAT IS DIFFICULT TO DO WITHOUT

Bamboo

At the time of writing bamboo (Tonkin) is readily available usually in 6'0" lengths. The quality of the material may well vary from pole to pole but over the years I have been only little troubled by poles of poor standard but if you are unlucky enough to come across a poor one then do not waste time working on it. By poor I mean one that has gouges cutting laterally across the fibres (splits that run down the length of the grain are usually of no consequence) or deep dark pits that will not be eliminated as the work progresses or of a generally mangy appearance. Even good poles can vary as can be illustrated by how they can differ in weight: for example, in the last order of bamboo I received the heaviest 6'0" one I weighed was 5lb 6ozs, the lightest was only a few ounces more than half that weight and the rest were around the 3½lb mark. The heaviest was the butt end of a culm and the lightest from the top end. Both were good clean-looking poles of

The culm to the right weighs 4lb 2oz, much the same as that for the Diary Rod and the ones used to produce the rods shown either side of it. These rods weigh about 4oz each which means there was a considerable quantity of dust and shaving 'lost' along the way

This sort of bamboo requires something more robust than a froe or a knife to split it

an even buff colour and comparable moisture content but the heavier one had great thick walls throughout whereas the other was altogether a more delicate item but still fine for the making of say an 8'0" #4 line size rod provided that care is taken to remove as few of the power fibres as possible. It is interesting to note that most of a pole, even a light one, will end up as shavings, dust or short end waste – the 5lb 6oz specimen will in all probability become a rod with two tops weighing in total about 6oz! In the past I was given some 12'0" culms some of which I still have and use for special projects such as one-piece rods.

TIP END WALL THICKNESS
1/4"
5/16"
BUTT.
2 1/4"

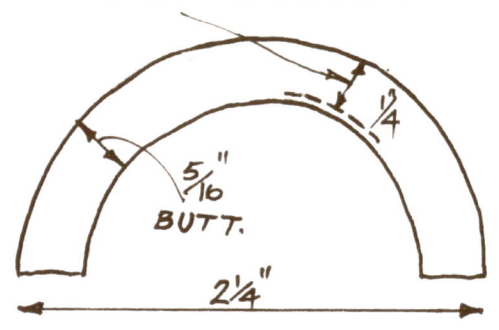

THE OUTLINE OF THE BUTT END OF THE POLE USED FOR THE ROD

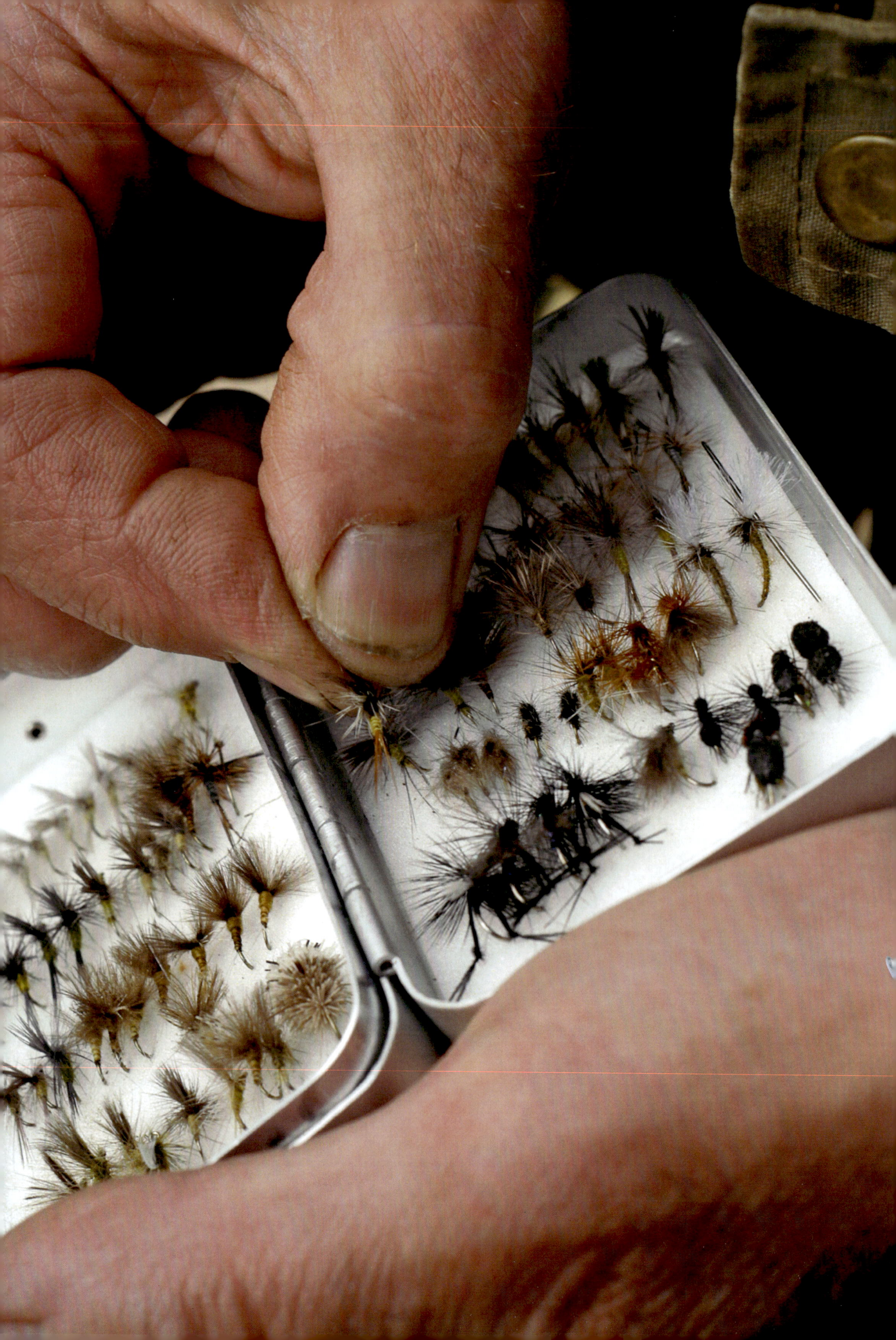

Session 2

Despite a considerable quantity of last night's torrential rain getting in under the workshop door a start was made today – a proper start and some rod making was done, when the poles were split into strips.

At one time I was pretty cavalier about this process, I would start at one end and drive a knife down the grain with a mallet and be delighted by the explosive pops it made as it burst its way through the nodes. Now I am more circumspect and start in the middle and work towards each end in turn which yields more strips and is less hazardous. Years ago the knife blade I was using broke and I cut a knuckle on the razor sharp edge of the bamboo which meant I had to spend ages in the hospital emergency department pretending to be far braver than I felt. I have since learned that head hunters in New Guinea used (let us hope the past tense is appropriate here!) bamboo knives to remove the desired part of their fallen enemies' anatomy. I now remind myself 'that compared with a neck a knuckle is nothing' and advise anyone splitting a pole to do the same.

The pole yielded 20 strips, which is about as many as I have ever got from a pole of this size and as many as I could sensibly have hoped for; 18 or 19 pieces are more usual numbers which still allow a butt and two tops to be made from the same pole. The extra lengths are therefore a bonus and in more ways than one as in addition to the obvious gain they will allow a spare spline to be made if a mistake is made.

The pole split quite truly and required little manipulation of the knife to keep the splits parallel and of a useful width. Sometimes a recalcitrant pole will split off at an angle and will require a fair bit of dexterity and experience to force it to yield a decent harvest of strips. As each strip was separated from the pole it was grouped with those from the same half of the pole which in theory at least should produce rod sections made from material that is as homogeneous as possible. I am fairly sure that such fastidiousness is in reality quite unnecessary, but as it takes no effort to arrange things in this fashion I do it just in case some benefit does accrue.

The final task was to stagger the nodes in the 12 strips that are to make the rod, trim away the waste and identify the spares as 'belonging' to this particular rod, for which I find the little tags used by gardeners for identifying plants to be ideal.

For years I have made rods with what I refer to as 'two node' coincidence (illustrated in the diagrams overleaf) rather than the three node system that is normally employed on manufactured rods. In theory this system should be the stronger method of construction and might have particular advantage in the finer parts of a rod though the three node coincidence makes perfectly fine rods and is less wasteful of bamboo.

When the staggering was done and the waste material had been cut off the strips were 54" long (the reason for the extra length will be explained in due course); the session, a short one, had lasted **45 minutes.**

THE 2 NODE COINCIDENCE USED IN THE DIARY ROD.

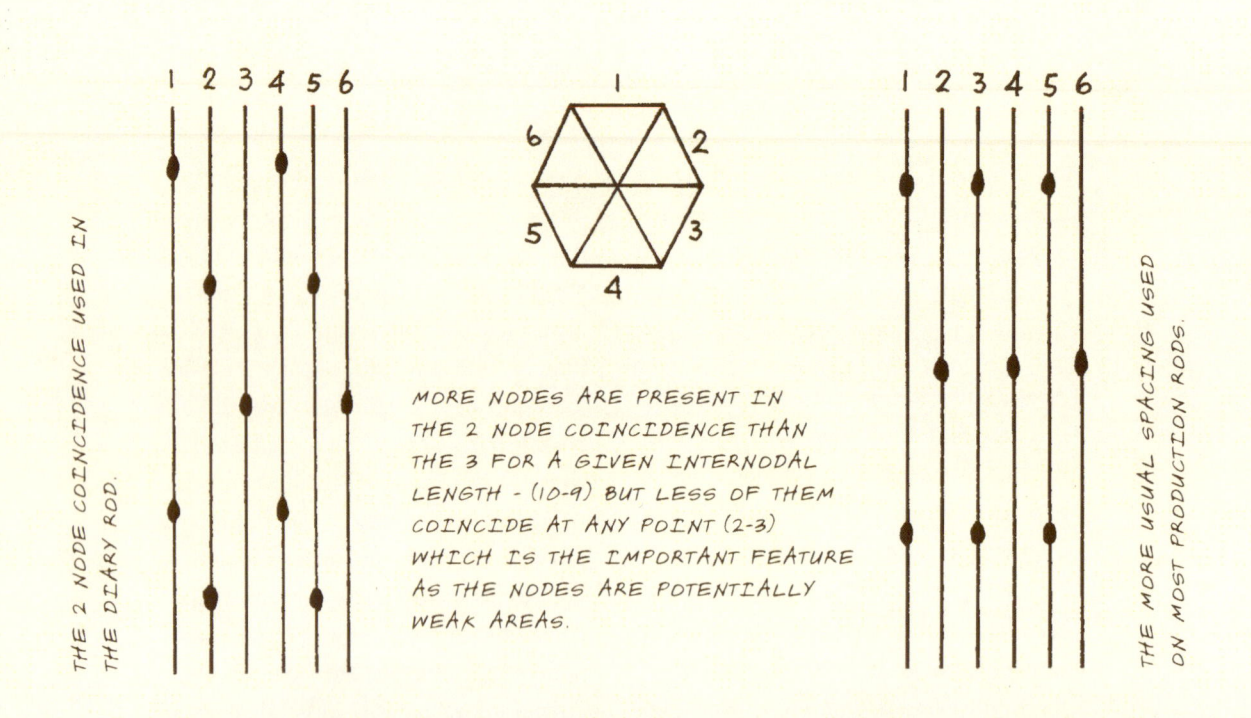

MORE NODES ARE PRESENT IN THE 2 NODE COINCIDENCE THAN THE 3 FOR A GIVEN INTERNODAL LENGTH - (10-9) BUT LESS OF THEM COINCIDE AT ANY POINT (2-3) WHICH IS THE IMPORTANT FEATURE AS THE NODES ARE POTENTIALLY WEAK AREAS.

THE MORE USUAL SPACING USED ON MOST PRODUCTION RODS.

Notes

Splitting

As may be ascertained from what is written above I use a knife to split the culm into strips and not a froe which is the tool specifically designed for the purpose. This is not because I have anything against this particular tool but simply because I have almost always used a knife and found it perfectly satisfactory. Indeed if I am perfectly frank I must admit that I have never used a custom-made froe though I did once 'doctor' a screwdriver for this purpose which I suppose comes near to being a froe.

OK FOR INITIAL HALVING BUT BEST AVOIDED THEREAFTER

A large firmer gouge – i.e. one bevelled outside to inside – is a good tool for knocking out the internal nodal divisions

What is useful advice however is that whatever tool is used to split a pole it is wise never to be too greedy and try to extract more strips from it than it is readily willing to produce. The result of this greed is almost always less strips than would otherwise have been the case; on any number of occasions I have believed that a rather wider than usual strip could be made into two usable thinner ones only to end up with none. It probably took me years to be cured of this misplaced optimism (and maybe the cure is not wholly complete even now!)

Initial split in middle of pole. Everything fairly standard here except possibly the use of a knife in place of a froe

However if you are desperate for an extra spline then you may succeed by starting the split from the inside (concave) rather than the outside face of the strip that, in your heart of hearts you know, is barely wide enough to make two. Indeed 'inside to outside' splitting is a perfectly satisfactory way of producing all the strips as it has the advantage of working from the culm's smaller (internal) circumference which may well cause one to be more realistic about how many strips it will produce. As a general rule I have found it easier to make good splines from strips that are on the 'full' rather than the narrow side, even though it takes a bit more work to reduce them to the required amount. To this end I try to produce strips at least ¼"+ wide even for the top sections of a rod.

Node staggering

Part of the interest and advantage of being an amateur is that one can experiment with differing ways of doing things without the pressures that a professional is subjected to in terms of producing quantities of rods and of making a living thereby. This element of the hobby seems to manifest itself to a greater and greater extent as time passes and numerous rods of standard design have been made – a bit of experimenting is interesting even when it is of a minor sort. For example, rods are occasionally made in which the nodes are completely staggered, i.e. none of them coincide, they spiral (in a helix) evenly up the rod, each successive node appearing on the 'next' face of the hexagon. To achieve this a culm with long internodal lengths of material is advantageous – nodes that are 16" or more apart. The downside of this method is that it is wasteful of material, usually producing ends of waste that are too short to be of much use.

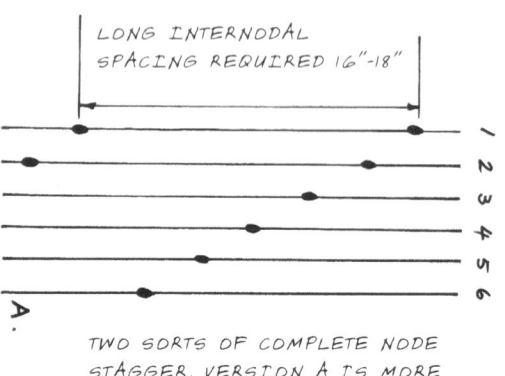

LONG INTERNODAL SPACING REQUIRED 16"-18"

A.

TWO SORTS OF COMPLETE NODE STAGGER, VERSION A IS MORE WASTEFUL OF MATERIAL THAN B, BUT IN THEORY AT LEAST IS MORE ROBUST/DESIRABLE

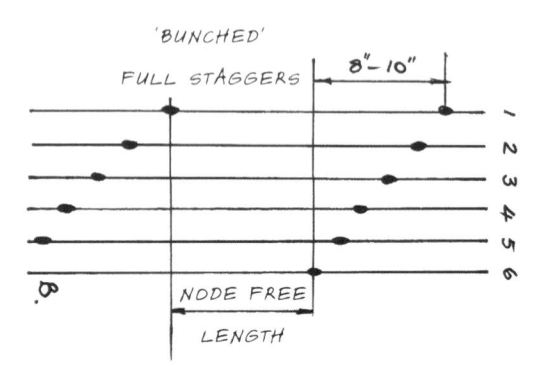

'BUNCHED' FULL STAGGERS 8"-10"

B.

NODE FREE LENGTH

An alternative to this long total stagger is to still have a complete stagger but in 'clusters' in which the nodes occupy a far shorter length of the rod section. For example, a 'long stagger' may be spread over 18" or whatever is the internodal spacing of the pole; the short one however may only occupy 8–9". This latter method was used to make some long (9'6") 2-piece rods for sea trout fishing some years ago as it allowed rod sections of up to about 60" to be made from a 6'0" pole. In the event the rods accounted for far more reservoir than sea trout but in doing so did not demonstrate any apparent weakness in respect of the node arrangement though my instincts incline me to think that it is a system that is best avoided.

Three 'odd' or 'incorrect' rods were also made about twenty years ago by way of experiment in which the node staggering was more or less random, at least to the point where no more than two nodes coincided precisely at any position on a section. One of these rods was given to a friend on condition that he used it in a fairly robust manner and the other two are still here with me. All three have been put through their paces with no obvious signs of weakness despite the haphazard node arrangements in the environments for which they were designed, i.e. one for river and the other two for sea and reservoir trouting. Each one has its modest tales to tell, tales that no doubt will be added to in the future.

Does this mean that there is greater leeway in respect of node staggering than is normally accepted or is it that three rods are not a sufficiently large sample to give valid data or that both these suppositions are correct? Despite my experiences with these rods I prefer the two node system used for the Diary Rod as I incline towards the belief that a planned and symmetrical arrangement must offer some advantages over the haphazard.

Splicing

Whereas some methods of arranging the nodes are wasteful of material one way of proceeding that allows shorter, otherwise useless, lengths to be utilised is by splicing together two (or more) pieces to produce a strip of the desired length. My experience with this has been with the butt sections of rods in which two of the splines have had one splice each in them. This was done because I was short of full length material and although normally I try to avoid the bother of splicing some rod makers produce rods that have the nodes wholly spliced out.

Again with splicing as with node staggering I have 'fiddled about' in as much as I have tried two methods, the first of which is the standard splice that is cut across the width of the two pieces to be joined. This is usually done with the aid of a splicing block that produces a joint some 4" long though I have made splices working entirely by eye which have been quite satisfactory; a block however makes things easier. The other type of splice was cut through the thickness of the cane inside to outside on one piece and vice versa on the other. This latter type was used on the butts of three or four rods which are still functioning well after many years of use. The trick, if it may be so described, with splicing is to ensure that the splice is long enough, there is a perfect union between the surfaces to be joined, the quality of the fibres either side of the glue line is comparable (best achieved by using material from the same pole) and that a meticulous bonding procedure is employed. With the second type of splice indicated above to ensure a perfect union of the areas to be joined the pieces were bound together on a strip of wood, the working surface of which was faced with a layer of hard rubber webbing as is the former when the laminations for a composite bow limb are bonded.

If splicing is resorted to then thought must be given to when the bamboo is to be tempered as the temperatures involved in this process may well cause a breakdown of the adhesive. If you are apprehensive about this then some test pieces need to experimented with. This can be easily done with short lengths in the kitchen oven set to 180°C for a period of 15–20 minutes. Indeed if many 'short ends' are going to be used to produce a wholly spliced rod section then they can all be tempered in the kitchen before being glued. Also when the strips have been spliced and are ready to be made into splines it might be wise to stagger the centre points of the splices as one would the nodes on a conventionally built rod, particularly if the top section of a rod is to be made in this way. This in turn may make one think that a splicing block with a shallower angle than the standard 4° is desirable which will lead to a longer overlap in the narrow splines.

A TYPICAL SPLICE OF THE SORT DESCRIBED

The working surfaces of the former for the bow limb and the Tonkin cane are lined with a hard rubber webbing, the slight 'give' in which ensures a perfect union between the surfaces being bonded

Clamps hold the components of the bow limb together whilst strips of rubber inner tube do the same to the cane

For the bonding procedure see Session 11

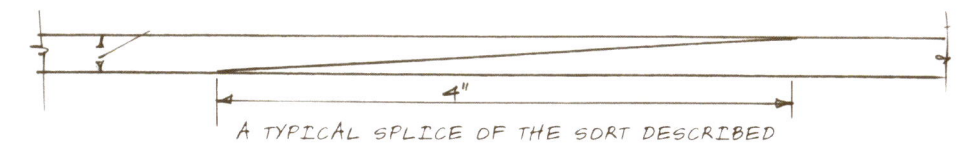

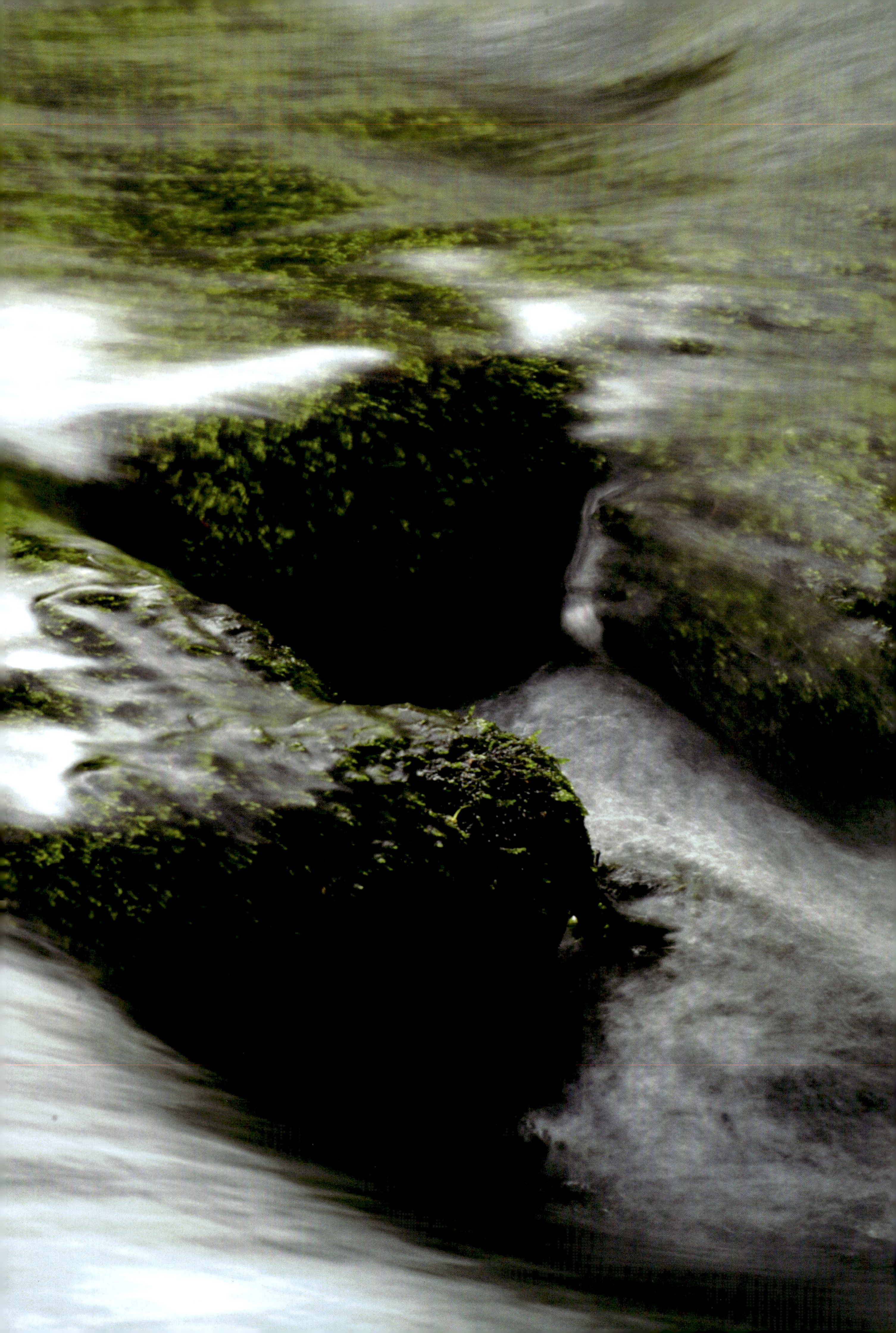

Session 3

Not all parts of the rod making process, or any craft work for that matter, are going to capture the imagination of the craft worker or demand great amounts of skill but are tasks that just have to be got through for the sake of the final product – a sort of delayed gratification in practical terms. Some parts of the rod making process can be difficult and sometimes seem to require rather more skill than is always readily available which of course can be a problem; today's work however fell into the first category.

Even though the pole split in a very well behaved fashion in the last session all the strips had to be straightened to some degree in this one, indeed one would have to be remarkably lucky not to have to do some correction. The main focus of the work had to be directed at the nodes where the material angled off from a straight line to a lesser or greater extent – a pole will sometimes split to give strips that look like arthritic fingers that go zig-zagging along and require quite some time and patience to rectify.

Today's pole was not like that I am pleased to say but of the 48 nodes in the two bundles 36 needed some work done on them. Not all these nodes will 'appear' in the rod sections because the strips at present are 54" long as was indicated previously but for the strips to be worked on properly all the nodes needed to be straight.

The bamboo was heated and so softened with a heat gun and then straightened with the clamping devices shown or by finger and thumb pressure. Typically a node area would be heated until it was just too hot to handle comfortably and then opposing pressure would be exerted and maintained until the bamboo was cool. The more noticeable curves or bends in the internodal lengths were similarly treated; whether this was strictly necessary is debatable but it will allow the strips to lie more comfortably in the grooved boards when the time for planing them comes. This repetitive business took me about 1½ hours to complete, after which I got on with the initial triangulation of each strip.

A HEAT GUN ALLOWS A CONTROLLED HEAT TO BE DIRECTED AT THE RELEVANT PART OF THE STRIP WITHOUT THE FEAR OF SCORCHING THE FIBRES

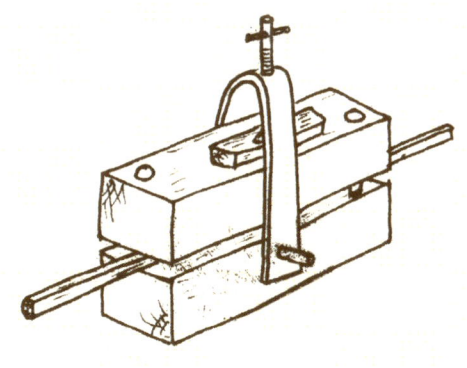

A FEW SIMPLE STIRRUP CLAMPS LIKE THIS ARE HELPFUL IN KEEPING THE PROCESS GOING AT A STEADY RATE

I have now come to a point where my rod making seems to deviate from all the methods I have heard or read about: with a sharp knife the edges of the essentially rectangular sectioned bamboo strips were trimmed away to create a triangular section that will locate directly in the 60° grooves of the preparation boards and make unnecessary the boards with asymmetrical grooves that can be used to prepare the cane for the 60° grooved board. Once some experience and a little confidence have been gained, the hand, eye and knife will work as one in a very co-ordinated way to produce triangulation that is surprisingly accurate with the inner apex of the section vertically opposite the side formed by the outside curve of the culm. The idea for this procedure came from bow making where it was not unusual for a bowyer to rough out the shape of a bow with a small sharp hand axe and/or a draw knife. A good knife will serve the same purpose for a rod maker.

(I wish we had the equivalent of bowyer in rod making. Maybe we should create a word, after all, Edward Lear created plenty and his were nonsense and so did Shakespeare but his were not, so how about rodder or rodyer?) Sorry about that but bowyer seems neater than bow maker.

Trimming the strips is not too long a job but when the time taken to accomplish it was added to that of node straightening the session had lasted **2 hours 25 minutes** and I was sitting amongst a very satisfying pile of bamboo splints.

REMOVING THE WASTE FROM A STAVE OF YEW WOOD. SOME CARE MUST BE EXERCISED BUT IT IS A QUICK EFFECTIVE WAY OF PROCEEDING

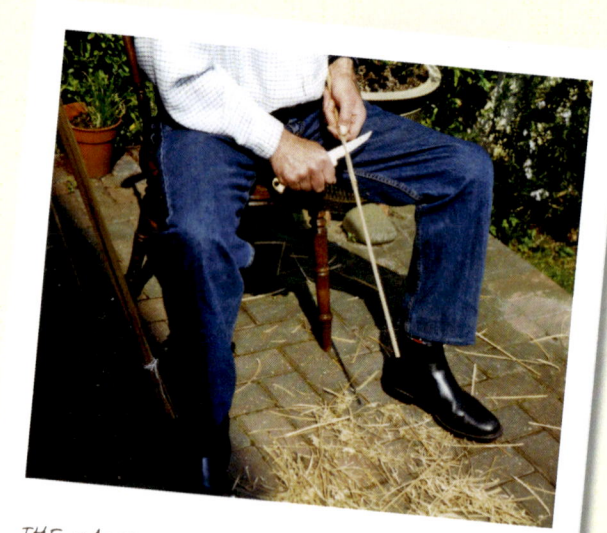

THE SAME PRINCIPLE BEING APPLIED TO A STRIP OF TONKIN

Six 'knife' triangulated strips (splines) bound together, one of which is subsequently shown located in the vee groove of the preparation board

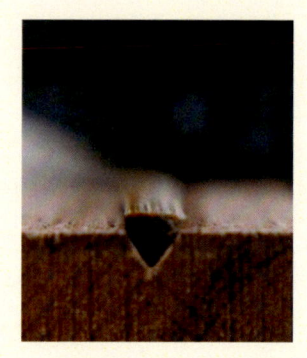

Notes

Node straightening

Even though node straightening is a straightforward operation in more senses than one some attention needs to be paid to it: an insufficiently heated node may emit a creaking sort of complaint as the straightening pressure is applied to it which may well mean that the fibres have been strained beyond their capabilities and are thus seriously weakened. If too much heat is applied the bamboo will char, harden and become brittle. In addition to the obvious consequences inherent in this the strips will be less pleasant to plane due to the varying hardness long their length and may be prone to tear at the hard parts. Also the dark colour caused by the excessive heat will emphasise the node positions in the rod – of course this may be to your liking though I try to avoid it. I suppose that it must be possible if one deals with hundreds of culms to come across one that splits into perfectly straight pieces – I think I am still waiting for this remarkable event to occur.

Occasionally it may be necessary to rectify faults in the nodes in addition to the straightening that has just been outlined. For example, nodes that protrude excessively above the surface of the surrounding cane may need to be pressed flat, or there may be 'dips' either side of some nodes that need to be brought level with the surrounding material. Both of these conditions need to be rectified. This can be done with heat and pressure to eliminate the necessity of removing too great a layer of power fibres both in terms of depth and length along the strip when the flat outside surface of the rod is being created.

All these procedures are carried out to ensure that as few power fibres as possible need be removed when fashioning the spline. This idea is well worth holding on to if one is going to exploit the full potential of a pole; it is a topic that I will return to on numerous occasions in the forthcoming pages and for which I make no apology.

THE AMOUNT OF 'OUTSIDE FIBRE' THAT HAS TO BE REMOVED TO CREATE A FLAT SURFACE WILL VARY ACCORDING TO THE SHAPE OF THE NODE AND ITS RELATIONSHIP TO THE SURROUNDING MATERIAL

LUMPY NODES SUCH AS THIS ONE MAY WELL REQUIRE HEATING AND PRESSING BEFORE BEING FILED FLUSH WITH THE SURROUNDING CANE

AN INSET NODE SUCH AS THIS, ALTHOUGH IT MAY APPEAR NEAT AND SMALL, MAY WELL REQUIRE TOO GREAT A LAYER OF FIBRES TO BE REMOVED TO EXPLOIT THE FULL POTENTIAL OF THE CANE

Initial triangulation

A good knife is one of the most useful tools imaginable, the one photographed (p. 28) was made to replace the one that broke all those years ago (see Session 2) as I had lost some confidence in boughten (a very useful and descriptive rural Gloucestershire word don't you think?) knives at that point. Its blade has shortened considerably with the passage of time due to all the sharpening required by such diverse jobs as carving bow centres, cleaning out dovetail joints, skinning deer and triangulating strips of bamboo of which it has done hundreds – pieces of bamboo, that is, not deer of which it has done only one. It could write a very interesting life story if it were so minded!

If the knife-triangulation seems a bit too bizarre then a pre-preparation board will have to be employed which need not be a terribly grand affair; one made from a good quality piece of softwood will suffice, made along the lines of the plan set out below which was the sort of thing I abandoned in favour of the knife.

A knife or a froe can be made, if one has the impulse to do so, from a piece of annealed high carbon steel or gauge plate that is a steel alloy which in addition to a high carbon content also has a host of other metals in its make-up. A strip $3/32$" thick can be shaped and drilled with ordinary workshop tools, heated with a blow torch and quenched in a bath of motor oil and then tempered in the kitchen oven set at about 200°C for an hour or so (if the cook will let you near it) before being finally quenched in the oil again. A bevel can be ground on with the workshop grinder before sharpening takes place on the oilstone; a froe may require rather thicker steel.

BY TRIANGULATING THE STRIPS WITH A KNIFE IT WAS POSSIBLE TO DISPENSE WITH THE VARIOUS SORTS OF PREPREPARATION BOARDS

BOARD WITH ASYMMETRICAL GROOVE

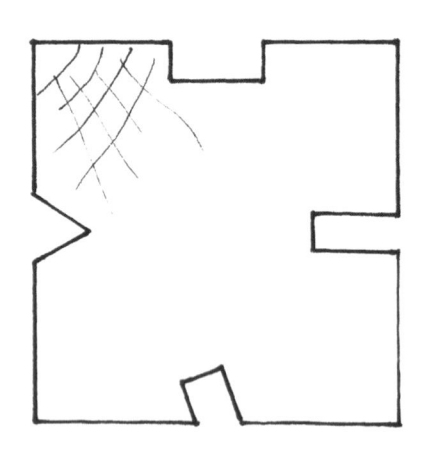

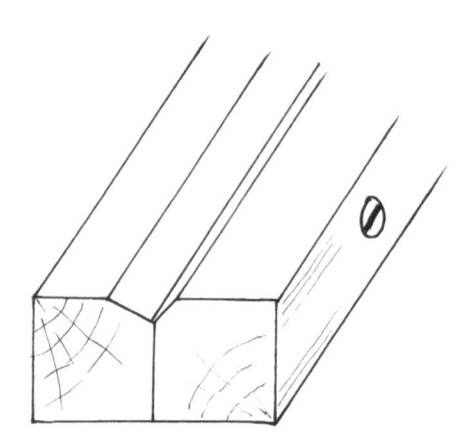

TWO TYPES OF ROUGH PLANING BOARDS, ONE ADJUSTABLE, THE OTHER 'SET'. THE SET BOARD IS THE TYPE USED BY RICHARD WALKER, THE ADJUSTABLE BY GARRISON

Session 4

This is the wrong time of the year to be in the workshop where conditions can be very Spartan as they are today – cold and dour, the sort of day that makes me envy those with well heated work areas. However as the workshop was out of commission in the more clement months the rod has to be made now if it is to be used in the warmth of spring and summer. From both a personal comfort point of view and from a practical angle I prefer to work when the weather is not extreme – very damp/very cold, etc. – as so many of the processes are then harder to complete satisfactorily and anyway this business is supposed to be fun.

This session's job was to rub down the protruding parts of the outside nodes level with the surrounding surface with the bamboo supported on the 'node anvil'. I used, initially, a bastard file which, incidentally, is the correct technical term for a file of this particular coarseness and not how I feel about it though sometimes (–!!) followed by abrasive paper. The job is quite simple but produces a very unpleasant dust that is composed mainly of the glass-like outer layer of the pole which really should not be inhaled or ingested, so all done up in my Darth Vader mask the nodes were reduced. These particular nodes were neat and even and did not stick out greatly or dip away where they merged with the material on either side so levelling them was easy enough. As I dealt with the nodes I speculated that whatsoever/whosoever created Tonkin cane did not have rod builders in mind – if they had, nodes would have been omitted whereupon an almost perfect natural rod making (and bow making) material would have been available. Maybe however that would be asking too much as what we have now is still very remarkable stuff.

The session lasted about *1 hour* which worked out at just less than 1½ minutes per node and as I finished I could hear a burble of sound from a distant Saturday afternoon football match, an evocative noise that I have heard many times when fishing for autumn grayling on various rivers whose flood plains make excellent flat pitches. It was a good omen on which to finish the session, which I did rather warmer than when I started.

NODE BEING REDUCED

Notes

Dust avoidance

In times gone by in places where bamboo was common it was used for a vast variety of jobs not all of them good: for example, one nefarious use was to shave the glass-like outer surface very finely and put it into the food of someone to be done away with where it acted as a most unpleasant abrasive causing the unfortunate recipient to make an early exit. We should take our cue from this when considering the dust we create in the workshop and do our best to avoid inhaling it to any extent over a long period of time. The best way to do this is to wear an effective filter mask of some sort and to regularly extract the dust from the workshop, ideally at the end of each session. I know that I am overly sensitive about this matter but having been brought up in a mining area before the days when coal dust was regarded as seriously as it should have been and seen young men become old before their time due to this neglect I do not feel that my sensitivity is misplaced. As time passes the dusts of more and more ordinary workshop materials that were formerly regarded as benign are being seen as health threatening.

A good airfilter mask is not a cheap item but is one of the best bits of kit that one can invest in if one intends to be involved in craft work of any sort for a prolonged period. A strange feature concerning this topic is that those whose chests are sensitive and easily irritated by short exposure to dust are more likely to take the necessary precautions than those who are not. Potential damage however is not dependent upon one's sensitivity in this respect. A friend of a friend who appeared immune to dust came to an untimely end due to his disregard of this important aspect of home workshop health and safety; effective dust extraction is a necessity not a luxury whatever craft activity one is engaged in.

An airfilter mask that will remove much harmful dust

Session 5

With the nodes flattened the roughly (knife) triangulated strips were ready to be planed in the 60° grooved preparation boards. At one time this initial planing was done in a short (30") board with parallel (even depth) grooves but I have moved on from there and now use long boards with tapered grooves which are more convenient on a number of counts: the strips can be clamped in place leaving both hands free, they do not have to be moved along the board and a degree of taper is imparted to them even at this early stage of the planing.

This initial planing was done with a jack plane which is ideal for quickly removing the roughness produced by the knife. As each inside face was planed flush with the board's surface it was marked LP (last planed) to ensure that the other face would be planed next, with the process being repeated until a respectable equilateral cross section was achieved which usually required that one face be planed once and the other twice. Throughout this procedure the outside surface was left strictly untouched and so still retained its slight curvature which will be flattened in due course. By planing each inside face alternately each spline will have a backbone of full-length fibres, the importance of which will be discussed soon. Eight strips were planed in this *1 hour 20 minute* session.

INITIAL PLANING WITH A JACK PLANE IN A LONG PREPARATION BOARD. THE SPLINE IS CLAMPED IN PLACE WITH A G. CLAMP THUS LEAVING BOTH HANDS FREE TO MANIPULATE THE PLANE

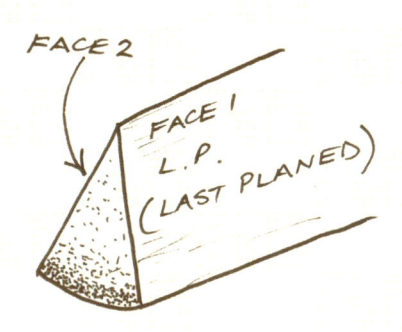

AS SOON AS FACE 1 HAS BEEN PLANED IT IS MARKED L.P. WHICH IS NOT ERASED UNTIL FACE 2 HAS BEEN PLANED. THE PROCESS IS REPEATED A COUPLE OF TIMES TO PRODUCE A SYMMETRICALLY FORMED SPLINE

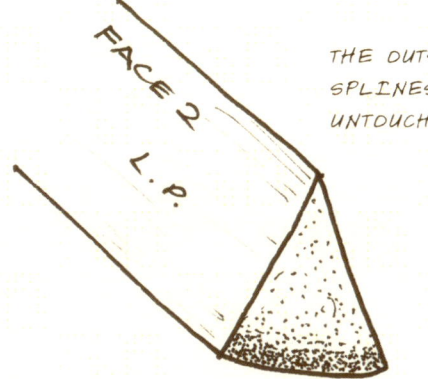

THE OUTSIDE CURVATURE OF THE SPLINES IS LEFT STRICTLY UNTOUCHED AT THIS STAGE

Notes

Preparation boards

A description of wooden grooved boards has already appeared in the section on methods of construction (page 10) along with a procedure for cutting the grooves; the tables below give the groove sizes that I have found convenient for preparing the cane for trout rods prior to them being planed in the adjustable metal boards. I am sure that other sizes and tapers would do equally well but these are offered as a starting point.

The 60° hand cutter being used to redress the groves in the long board

These boards need not be made of hardwood though if they are they will be more durable than those made from softwood. Whatever the hardness of the chosen wood care will have to be exercised in its use otherwise the quality of the splines produced in it will reduce over time. Strange as it may sound it is perfectly feasible to plane hundreds of splines without wrecking a board's surface if one learns to 'float' the plane over its surface as the cane is being reduced. I cannot find another word that expresses the action that is better than float – where the weight of the tool rather than the force of one's arm does the cutting. There are of course some practical things that can be done which reduce the chances of spoiling a board, e.g. setting the plane iron so that it protrudes evenly and not too much from the sole, putting a cross hatching of pencil marks over the board's surface so that any material removed is immediately apparent, keeping the sole of the plane in the same plane as the grooved surface and finally (maybe the most important) using some imagination in respect of what is taking place. Even when heed is paid to all these factors however there will come a time when a board will need to be redressed.

GROOVE SIZES (DEPTHS)

TAPERED GROOVES 60" BOARD

GROOVE	FROM	TO
1	1/16"	1/4"
2	3/16"	3/8"
3	3/8"	1/2"

A SELECTION OF GROOVES THAT SHOULD ALLOW SPLINES FOR A VARIETY OF RODS TO BE PREPARED FOR THE ADJUSTABLE BOARDS

PARALLEL (EVEN DEPTH) GROOVES BOARD

GROOVE	DEPTH	GROOVE	DEPTH
1	1/8"	4	5/16"
2	3/16"	5	3/8"
3	1/4"	6	1/2"

Session 6

I felt lively this morning despite the cold workshop so that in about ¾ hour the remaining four splines were planed which meant that all twelve splines were ready to have the curvature of their outside faces flattened. This was done with a 'spoke shave' type of cabinet scraper whilst a spline was located in a groove that allowed just the crown of the curve to protrude marginally above the surface and so be removed.

This is my preferred method of doing this job because the handles of the tool enable one to keep the cut parallel to the board's surface and so produce a 'flat' that is positioned symmetrically opposite the inner apex of the spline.

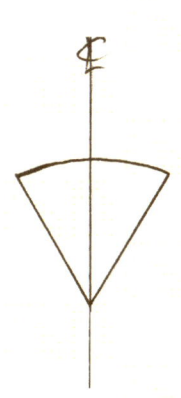

THE INNER APEX OF A SPLINE SHOULD BE SYMMETRICALLY OPPOSITE THE CENTRE POINT OF THE OUTSIDE CURVATURE TO PRODUCE AN ITEM THAT WORKS TO ITS MAXIMUM EFFICIENCY WITH AN EVEN DISTRIBUTION OF POWER FIBRES ABOUT THE AXIS

As an alternative this task will occasionally be accomplished with abrasive paper wrapped around a cork block. When the flattening was complete the outside corners were still slightly rounded but this did not matter as these features will disappear and become angular in the subsequent planing operations. This is the most satisfactory way I have found of retaining the greatest amount of power (outside) fibres though whether one needs to be so fussy is open to question but it does make me feel that I am going with the principle of retaining as many of them as possible.

The session overall was quite short lasting only *1 hour 50 minutes.*

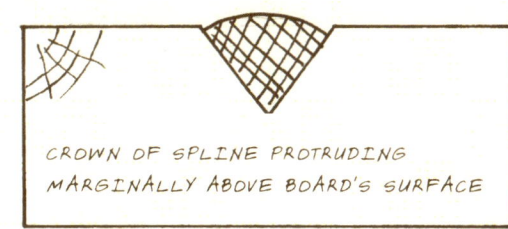

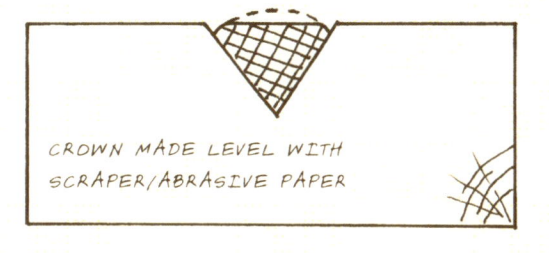

CROWN OF SPLINE PROTRUDING MARGINALLY ABOVE BOARD'S SURFACE

CROWN MADE LEVEL WITH SCRAPER/ABRASIVE PAPER

SUBSEQUENT PLANING OF INSIDE FACES WILL LEAVE FINAL SPLINE WITH SHARPLY DEFINED EDGES

Notes

Treatment of the outside surface of the splines

When I started rod making I was lucky enough to receive much excellent advice from the late Richard Walker who in completely unsolicited manner responded to a letter of mine that he saw in an angling magazine. Some of this advice related to power fibre removal even the thought of which he convinced me should be regarded as a sort of heresy of the worst kind. In keeping with this edict I made some rods from splines that had their outside surfaces untouched apart from the node reduction. One of these I still possess and although it does not look cosmetically very great and is probably also 'dimensionally challenged'(!) it still works well and there does not appear to have been a diminution in its powers after many years of use. It would not really be possible to make and sell such rods as there is an entirely reasonable expectation amongst purchasers that a rod should look elegant as well as perform well, however the amateur rod maker need not be always constrained by such considerations. If a culm of large diameter is used in the way just described then the curvature of the outside faces of the splines will be minimal, even the wide ones in the butt of the rod, and if the pole is also of fine appearance cosmetically then the finished rod may well look very respectable. In more or less complete contrast to this I am certain that it is not a good idea to sacrifice too great a quantity of power fibre on the twin altars of cosmetic perfection and exact minute dimensional precision that seem to obsess some people.

At a purely practical level for the amateur, who is unlikely to have access to the same choice of poles as the professional, the more or less total retention of power fibre may well allow him to make a rod that is as good or better from a slightly inferior (thinnish walled) pole than someone who starts with a first class culm and kills its potential by removing an excessive layer of such fibres as the outside material of the former will be better than the deeper layers of the latter.

In pursuit of the same principle of leaving the power fibres in as untouched a state as possible I have never been tempted to 'decorate' a rod by say flaming if for no other reason than that having taken ages to make it I am disinclined to set light to it. I accept that the cosmetic appearance of the process appeals to some but the principle of leaving the surface of any item that is to be subjected to great tension in as uncompromised a state as possible is one that is best adhered to. A rod that has its surface nicked by say a hook strike or maybe over enthusiastic 'decoration' is far more likely to be subject to progressive or sudden failure starting at the point where it has been weakened. Wooden bows suffer from the same frailty so archers go to great lengths to keep particularly the backs of their bows which are under great tension when the bow is drawn as unblemished as possible and I think fly fishers should do the same with their fly rods which makes me feel that flaming is best avoided.

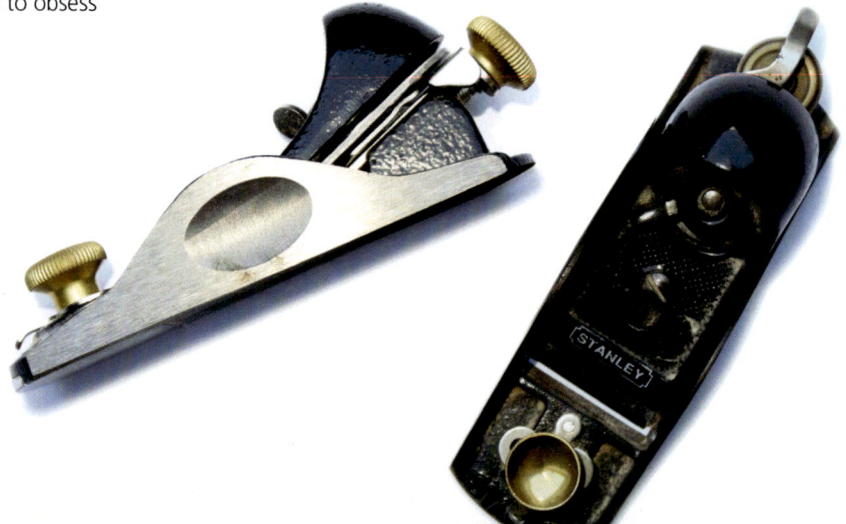

Session 7

The first job today was to set the adjustable steel board for the butt splines; the board has two grooves, one on each side, one of which is larger than the other by a few thousandths of an inch. By setting the smaller of the groves to the required size the other automatically becomes suitable for the penultimate planing of the splines.

Setting a board is a job that always takes longer than anticipated, rather like those mere 10 minute household jobs that in reality never take less than 60 to complete. It always seems such a simple idea to slide the appropriately sized 'gauge spline' of cane under my rather nice ebony wood straight edge held tight to the board's surface whilst the adjustment screws are tightened or loosened until it just 'catches' at the required point. The fact is however that it is far easier to make the adjustment just too small or that little bit too big so there is much fiddling about accompanied by the compulsory amount of huffing and puffing. Today I got there in the end but it did take far longer than I had allowed for which was not helpful as I had gone AWOL from some fence repairing and shopping, though quite how I was manoeuvred into two such activities on one day is a mystery but one that will doubtless occur again regardless of any evasive action I may employ! Before the first of the splines was worked on a test spline was planed and measured with that most essential of tools, the micrometer.

Despite all the mundane 'home' demands all six splines were planed with a sharp ironed block plane in the larger of the two grooves and then bound tightly together in readiness for being tempered in a later session, after which it was on with digging the fence post holes, having spent about **1½ hours** at rod making.

SETTING A BOARD BY DRAWING A TEST SPLINE UNDER A STRAIGHT EDGE HELD TIGHT TO THE SURFACE, WHEN CORRECTLY SET THE SIZE IS NOTED ON THE BOARD'S SIDE

SIZE RECORDED ON WOODEN ADJUSTABLE BOARD

Notes

Planing in the grooves – metal and wood

I keep a selection of old splines that for some reason or other were not suitable for the rod for which they were made maybe because they had an unsightly blemish that could not be eradicated or a slight tear in the grain. By planing one of these and checking it for accuracy any discrepancy in the setting of the board is quickly and painlessly exposed and can be rectified before the 'real' splines are planed. Such caution is not usually necessary but occasionally a setting will need tweaking. I suppose that it is a 'belt and braces' approach but one that puts my mind to rest and so keeps me happy. I have never employed a DTI (dial test indicator) for setting the metal boards though I am sure that it is an excellent method once one is used to it.

Even after using metal boards for a long time now I still remain surprised that a block plane designed for use with wood will happily shave fine shims off their mild steel surface or indeed gouge out chunks if canted at an angle. When I started using boards of this sort I imagined that they would be more or less impervious to the attentions of the blade but nothing could be farther from the truth. Of course a bit of thought on my part would have removed my surprise as before the advent of the high speed steel or tungsten carbide cutters that are available today the high carbon steel that block plane blades are made from would have been employed to shape an item from steel of the sort from which the boards are made. So, just as a plane has to be 'floated' on a wooden board so it has over one of steel. Over time a metal board will be reduced but, within certain limits, this is not harmful provided the reduction occurs evenly over the whole surface, and of course it can be redressed in the appropriate manner if you feel the wear is excessive or uneven. After a long session one ends up with quite a bit of 'steel dust'. In fact there always seems to be rather more of this metallic dust than there is wood dust when a rod is made in a wooden former and maybe in some mysterious way this is the case as a carefully used wooden board will turn out similarly sized splines for dozens of rods over years of time – all rather strange and unexpected.

Session 8

Today's session was essentially a repeat of Session 7 except that it was the splines for the rod's top section that were reduced after the board with the finer grooves had been set, though this time my expectations about the time it would take to set the grooves were more realistic, so when it took 'only' 30 minutes I felt quite pleased with myself. It was also the session in which the first mistake was made when the grain on one spline not so much tore as splintered because I was trying to squeeze a bit of extra mileage out of a plane blade that should have been sharpened a spline or so earlier. It is a fault of mine that when things are going OK I tend to press on rather than disturb the rhythm of the work despite knowing quite well that really I should stop and rectify the situation. It is a daft habit and one I should try to control, but I always think I can finish just one more spline before having to go through the rigmarole of sharpening the blade, cleaning off the oil, washing my hands and then resetting the cut which never seems quite so well adjusted as formerly. Despite all my resolutions I doubt if I'll change much as usually I get away with it! The extra spline was quickly made from one of the spare strips that was set aside for just such an eventuality.

When six perfect splines had been made they were bound tightly together with strong linen thread in readiness for being tempered which will be the next part of the process.

At this stage both sections are still 54" long which is (obviously) longer than will be required for half an 8'0" rod.

Making the extra spline made for a longer session than anticipated – *2 hours* – but I accepted this as an appropriate sanction for being slipshod.

A Diary Rod will also work quite well in the dark!

Notes

Unpleasant surprises when planing

Despite my occasional shortcomings in respect of blade sharpening there are some things that I do try to stick to very carefully – for example, it is always advisable to plane the spline away from the point at which it is secured to the grooved board whether this is done with a clamp or the hand as this eliminates the chances of buckling it in a terminal fashion between the forward thrust of the plane and the immovable clamp – immovable objects and unstoppable forces, etc. etc.

Even when one proceeds sensibly there can still be some potentially unpleasant surprises lying in ambush however cautious the approach is to planing. These will fray the temper of the craftsman and the bamboo and include, for example, catching the cuff of your sleeve in the near end of a spline as the plane is moved forward, or having a shaving fail to break off as the plane is lifted at the end of a forward stroke and withdrawn in readiness for the next pass down the spline. I know these things to be so because over the years they have occasionally leapt up and startled me and unless I am very vigilant will do so again in the future, I dare say. However, if you proceed with rather more caution than I can always muster should you get around to making a rod I am sure you will avoid having to make extra splines on a regular basis.

Sometimes one's past experience with other 'woodworking' crafts will be found to be non applicable. For example, when working with most woods it is almost invariably fatal to plane a tapered item from the thin end towards the thick if one harbours any hopes of producing an aesthetic looking smooth surface as the grain will almost invariably tear. So, taking my cue from this I avoided doing the same with bamboo only to subsequently find that provided one proceeds with care cane is perfectly forgiving of being planed in this 'wrong' way. This has proved very helpful when reducing say the last foot or so of the thick end of a spline which is where the clamp is initially placed to allow the plane to move towards the tip in an unimpeded manner over the majority of the spline's length. The clamp can safely be moved to a midway point when the thinner portion has been reduced thus allowing the plane be moved in the opposite direction towards the thick (butt) end without penalty – all very convenient because it is not possible to plane the cane immediately adjacent to the clamping point. It is however wise to carry out this operation with a bit of imagination particularly over a node so as not to tempt fate to too great a degree.

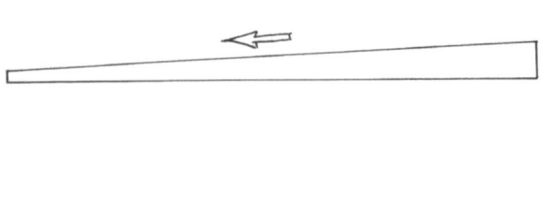

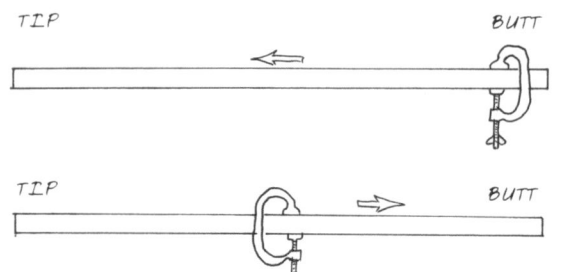

NORMALLY IT IS ESSENTIAL WITH MOST NATURAL MATERIALS TO PLANE IN THE DIRECTION OF THE ARROW I.E. DOWN THE SLOPE TOWARDS THE THIN END OF THE WORK IF ONE HAS ANY INTENTION OF AVOIDING THE GRAIN FROM TEARING. BAMBOO HOWEVER IS VERY FORGIVING IN THIS RESPECT AND WILL ALLOW ONE TO PLANE IN THE 'WRONG' DIRECTION AND STILL PRODUCE A FINE UNTORN SURFACE

MOST OF A SPLINE WILL BE PLANED IN THE DIRECTION INDICATED HERE – DOWN THE SLOPE AND AWAY FROM THE CLAMPING POSITION

MOVE THE CLAMP TO PLANE THE THICK END OF THE SPLINE

Session 9

Today the splines for both sections of the rod were tempered in a heavily insulated double 'tube' oven rectangular in section stopped at one end by a removable 'lid', open at the other and divided for almost the whole of its length as illustrated. Hot air from a 2 kilowatt heat gun is blown in through one tube and back through the other in which the sections are positioned on a mesh shelf to create a temperature of about 180°C. Once the oven was up to temperature the top section was in for 12 minutes and the butt for 17, the difference in time being advisable because of their differing diameters/mass.

When the sections were put into the oven they were tightly bound together with linen thread to prevent the heat from reactivating the plastic memory in the cane and so reintroducing into the splines the angles and curves that were so painstakingly removed a few sessions ago. For the same sort of reason the sections were checked for bends and twists as I did not want such defects 'fixed' by the heat and have to be subsequently removed. Linen was used because a synthetic thread, say nylon, might not withstand the curing temperatures. The diameters of the sections at this stage were about 10 thou greater than the required final size which allowed for the loss in dimension occasioned by the tempering process but would still leave some material to be removed in the final planing operation.

When the splines were removed from the oven the bindings were found to be quite slack due to the shrinkage caused by water loss and the possible drying out of the natural oils, etc. found in bamboo. Even apparently bone dry bamboo will contain a certain amount of moisture so the tempered splines instead of being about 10 thou bigger than final size were now about 6/7 thou larger than the rod size, an amount I find ideal for removal in the final planing operation, and their colour a shade or so darker but not greatly so. The heat will also have hardened the cane, made the fibres more steely and brittle which will have to be paid heed to when they are next planed.

Lying flat on the bench the splines cooled quickly and whilst they were doing so the block plane blades were sharpened as particularly keen irons would be now required for the hardened material. I dealt with the splines for the top section today, the butt ends of which were carefully positioned and clamped at the relevant point in the finishing groove, planed flush with the board's surface and checked with the micrometer. All went well and I ended up with six neatly planed splines that fitted together well when bound with strong cotton thread, at which point *1¾ hours* had elapsed.

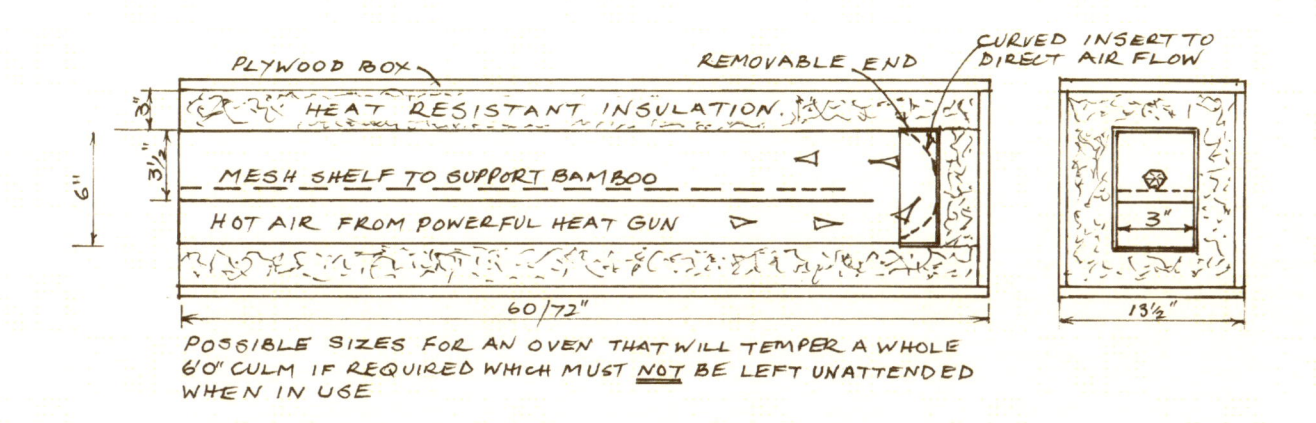

Notes

Tempering the cane – various methods

The question of heat treating is one that exercises the minds of rod makers to a considerable extent and includes, for example, such points as the best temperatures and times to employ, when to temper, what exactly happens when tempering occurs, etc. etc. My opinions on this process are quite ambivalent apart maybe from the obvious thoughts that some degree of tempering is beneficial if only to drive out excess moisture, that very high temperatures allied with long curing times are probably best avoided and that there seem to be a number of ways in which tempering can be achieved, all of which can lead to good rods. I have tried various ways of tempering and although I now usually adopt the method set out above I will sometimes employ one or other of the procedures indicated below as the mood takes me.

The culm can be tempered at the outset of the rod making process which is the method I used in making the first few dozen rods. The culms were split into halves and the heating was done with a standard gas blow torch which was played back and forth on both the inside and outside surfaces of the bamboo during which it was not allowed to dwell at any stage of its travel. As the cane became hot little jets of steam would begin to issue from the end grain and if the pole was a particularly wet one drops of liquid would fall to the floor which gave rise in the past to the rather euphemistic but apt expression of 'arousing the moisture'. Provided the heating continued steadily and evenly over the whole pole the colour would darken and the jets of steam would gradually cease. This I took to indicate that the bamboo was sufficiently dried out. The workshop would also have filled with a distinctive but not unpleasant smell which once experienced is unlikely to be forgotten – it always reminds me of the elephant house at the local zoo, a strange association I have to admit. It is also possible to temper the strips of bamboo directly after they have been split from the parent pole in the L shaped frame that is described in the next paragraph. The amount of dead weight in liquid form that a pole can contain is considerable, weight that will dull a rod's performance just as excessive moisture in a bow stave will lead to a sluggish and indifferent weapon unless it is removed. In reality complete elimination is probably neither possible nor desirable – if a moisture content of say 10 or 12% is achieved and maintained then all will be well. What other constituent parts of the bamboo (natural oils, pectins, etc.) are driven off during the process I have no way of telling and can only suppose that some are likely to evaporate particularly if very high temperatures are employed. As a procedure 'tempering first' has both pros and cons, one advantage being that the splines have to be bound together only once for gluing rather than for both tempering and then gluing. The disadvantages include having to plane hardened cane during each planing operation along with the necessity of storing the bamboo in a very dry place to stop reabsorption of water and if a blow torch is used the scorching mentioned above must be avoided.

Another method involves tempering the oversized sections before they are planed to final size (one at a time) in an L shaped frame (lined with silver foil if you wish) where they are held by a series of cup hooks as the heat gun is played over them during which they receive heat directly from the gun and the back draught from the frame. After each couple of passes along the length the section is rotated to present a different face to the heat with the thicker parts receiving more heat time than the finer ones. No temperatures are taken but if one proceeds cautiously when one first uses the method experience will soon be gained and it will be discovered that it is a perfectly good way of producing a rod full of vitality. I have to admit that I sometimes use this method even though a more sophisticated system is available as I am able to instantly proceed with minimum of fuss without having to get the pipe oven out from its living space which could be a sign of laziness or impatience or indeed both.

I did try using an oven as described in Garrison and Carmichael and got as far as obtaining a 4" diameter cast iron pipe and constructing a long gas multi-holed jet burner but the whole affair was so heavy, cumbersome and space consuming in addition to which it took an age to 'fire up' that I sort of lost interest in it and put the time and effort employed in the project down to experience, but do not let me put off those of you with larger workshops than mine and bit more patience as the system can obviously work well. There is also an illustration of another sort of pipe oven below made from a 7'0" length of copper pipe lagged to reduce heat loss which works tolerably well that was made when, more by chance than design, I obtained a pipe of this length.

For those of an inquisitive nature the effects of differing curing temperatures and times can be ascertained by baking similarly sized strips in a kitchen oven where both variables can be precisely controlled. The test pieces can then be subjected to whatever tests you think appropriate, e.g. degree of flexing, number of flexings, etc., maybe whilst propelling an object such as a marble to add a bit more interest to the process. From this the amount of 'set' can be measured after a given number of repetitions and colour variations noted, which may prove useful for those who intend to temper their rods according to such colour change using the same principle as that formerly employed to ascertain the temper of an object made from high carbon steel. The likelihood is that you will arrive at the same conclusions as other rod makers but this does not matter as you will have had the fun and gained the experience of conducting the tests. Many years ago a group of young people conducted similar sorts of tests on various types of wood to determine which would be the best for making an archery bow and in so doing learned far more than they would by simply getting the information from books and neither would they have received the congratulations of the university engineering staff to whom they demonstrated their project.

Finally you can of course make a decent rod from untempered bamboo provided it has been thoroughly dried out by being kept in a very warm place for a good length of time. Such a rod may take a bit more of a set than a conventional one and may not have such a crisp action but it will be as tough as rope and will be a very durable item. I once stored some poles for many months in an industrial boiler room that was desiccatingly hot and dry and then made a few untempered rods with them which have worked well ever since, indeed their performance is not noticeably different from similar types of rods that received conventional heat treatment. This made me wonder whether a long low level of heat does not in fact effect some degree of tempering just as a slow cooker does with say vegetables – the water never boils but the food does cook.

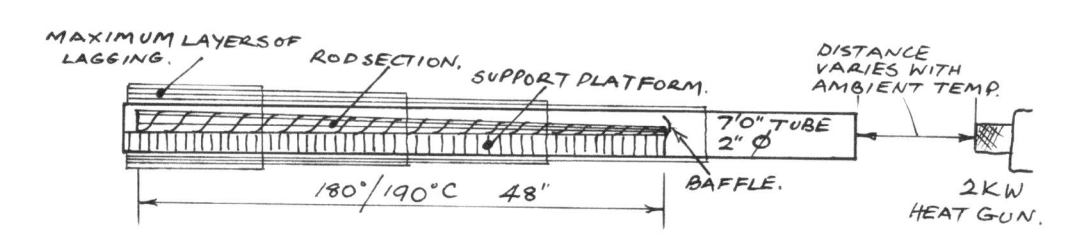

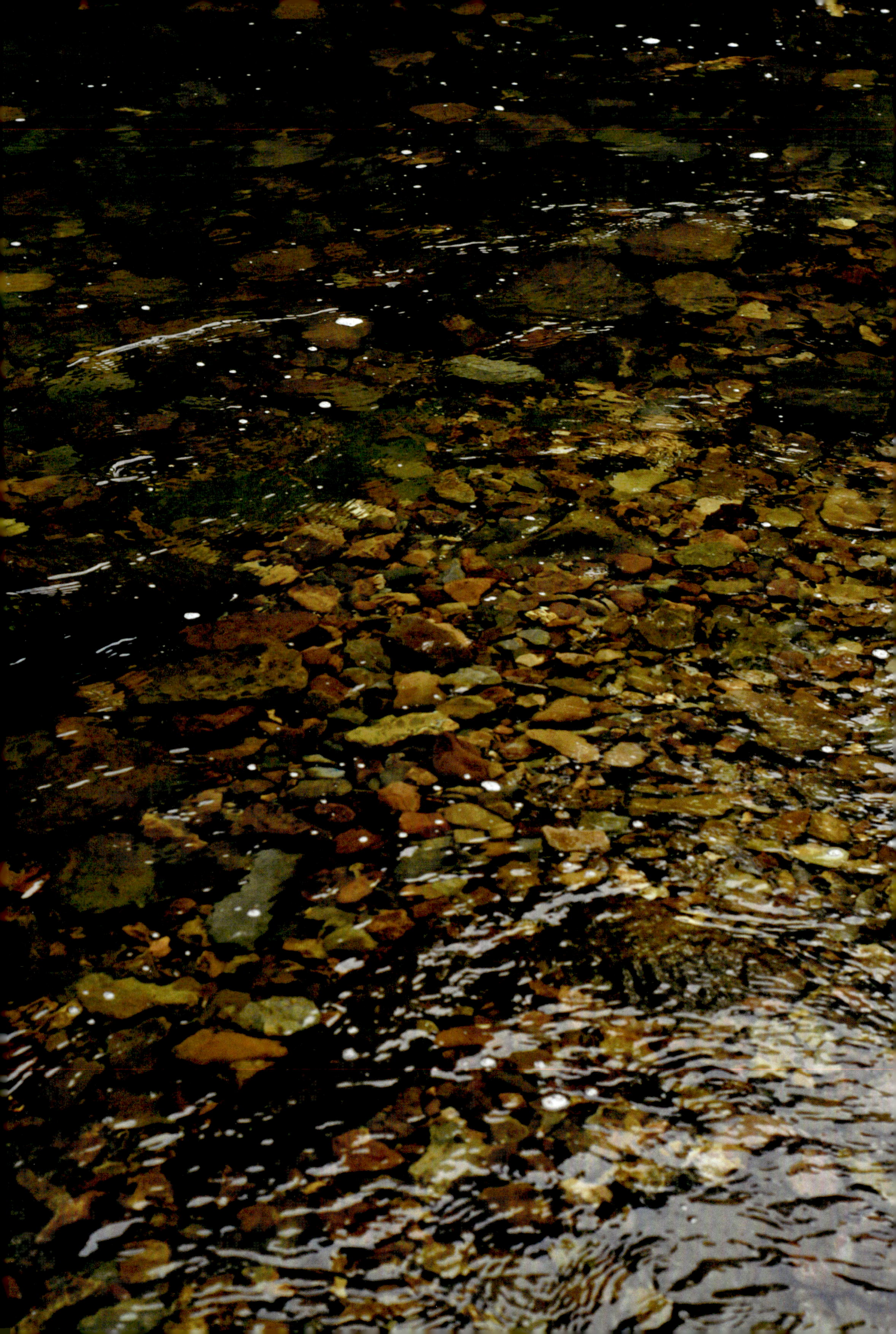

Session 10

Today the butt splines were planed to their final size as were those for the top in the last session. I very nearly had another crisis on my hands when a jack plane, of its own volition, leapt on to a spline and bruised it. Luck was with me however as it made only the merest dimple on the very end of the thick part of the spline where it will be covered by the reel seat. You will just have to believe me when I say that it is most unusual for me to make two errors of this type but that is the case, even though I daydream at times. Maybe someone/something is testing my promise to record everything about the making of this rod, a promise I wish I had not made just at the moment! There are sometimes minor wobbles along the rod making path but I rarely fall off to the extent of having to make two new or even one extra spline for that matter.

Once the planing was over the splines were checked for size at various points along their length with the micrometer and then bound together for safety, i.e. to prevent the crisp edges of the cane from becoming dulled or otherwise harmed and then put in a warm dry place in readiness for gluing.

The job is 80% complete now I reckon and although what has yet to come has to be competently done the essential core of the task is over; good, well formed and accurately dimensioned splines will lead to an effective rod whereas poor ones will at best produce an indifferent item that is likely to fail at some crucial moment. By now the session had lasted *1½ hours.*

Notes

Measurements and grain structure

The measurements of the splines were within quite acceptable tolerances, with deviations of just the odd thou here and there which concerned me not in the least degree and is a topic I will comment on in the pages to come. Each spline has full length grain running down its backbone (long axis), a feature that should influence the performance and durability of the rod and one that was purposely created through a combination of the initial straightening of nodes, etc. and by planing each inside face of the splines alternately. In addition to this full length grain the grain structure within a spline will exhibit a symmetrical quality that is best explained by the illustration below. Good wooden bows and arrows will exhibit the same qualities although unbroken end to end grain is an elusive quality in the best bow woods, notably yew, though perversely it is quite a common feature in woods of less stature. It took me ages, years actually, to find a yew tree from which I could cut some 6 foot staves, one of which was made into the 50lb bow shown here. In the great scheme of things it is not a first class bow as the wood did not have such bow 'in it' but it did allow me to fulfil the modest ambition of making such an item from felling the tree to shooting an arrow, though having written this it will propel a field arrow on average 140/150 yards which would be/is plenty far enough to cause mischief! Nevertheless I hope this rod will perform its tasks rather better than the bow. Perhaps if the wood like the bamboo had come from half way round the world there would be more parity in their respective performances as the best yew wood generally comes from Oregon in western USA.

A DIAGRAMMATICAL REPRESENTATION OF HOW THE GRAIN IN A SPLINE (OR BOW LIMB. SEE RIGHT FOR A FLAT BOW PROFILE) SHOULD 'FADE OUT' SYMMETRICALLY ALONG ITS LENGTH AND HOW THERE SHOULD BE SOME FULL LENGTH FIBRES FORMING A BACKBONE. SUCH AN ARRANGEMENT WILL 1) EXPLOIT THE MATERIAL'S FULL POTENTIAL 2) PRODUCE A DURABLE ITEM AND 3) REDUCE THE TENDENCY FOR THE ROD TO 'KICK OFF' OUT OF THE DESIRED PLANE OF ACTION. GOOD STRAIGHTENING AND THE PLANING OF EACH INSIDE FACE ALTERNATELY WILL GO A GOOD WAY TO ENSURING THAT THIS GRAIN STRUCTURE PERTAINS

Session 11

Many years after I started rod making I got around to making a binding device for securing the splines prior to tempering them and during the bonding process. It took me some time to make the item because I had always succeeded in binding the sections by hand so working on the principal of 'if it ain't bust don't fix it' I let things stand. Nowadays however I usually use the binder but in this instance – maybe just for the record or old times' sake – I reverted to hand binding if for no other reason than to illustrate that it can be done in this fashion.

Be all that as it may however before the gluing took place the inside surfaces of each spline that were to receive the adhesive were lightly scored with fine glass-paper and degreased with acetone. Abrading and degreasing are standard practices when a modern composite bow is made because, just as with built cane rods, it is only the adhesive that holds the components together; the transference of ideas such as this from the one craft to another is something I find useful and interesting. Grease and dirt are the enemies of successful adhesion and so must be eliminated as far as practically possible which is where the acetone comes in. The splines were not dirty or greasy in any normal sense but even the natural finger grease that is inevitably transferred when they are handled is best eliminated.

The scoring increases the area, albeit by a small amount, to which the glue can adhere and adds a bit of mechanical interlocking to the adsorbtion and absorption that are features of the gluing process. Turkish bowyers of old had a tool called a tashin, a sort of fine toothed steel scraper, with which they scored the wood and horn laminates that along with sinew were used to make wonderful bows, the best of which would shoot a flight (distance) arrow up to half a mile; rod makers however can make do with a bit of glass paper. In bow making such fastidiousness is not misplaced as a bow that fails at full draw is very dangerous, sending jagged bits of limb going in all directions around the archer's head; at least if a rod fails it is only heartache for the lost rod section and the (inevitably) good fish that will occur.

About half a cup of Cascamite One Shot glue was mixed according to the manufacturer's instructions and then poured into a 1" diameter plastic pipe that had been cut lengthways to create a trough long enough for the spines to lie completely in it. First the butt splines were put in and thoroughly soaked in glue with the help of a stiff bristled artist's brush. This left them in a very sticky state to handle which however is far preferable to having dry spots (glue free) that could cause rod failure. The binding set up was as illustrated in the photographs overleaf with me sitting in front of a reel from which thread was drawn and wound on to the splines, the drag on the reel having been set at about 1½ lbs of pressure. Before binding the splines were arranged according to their numbering (1–6) which ensured that the node staggering would be correct. Initially the section was bound tightly for about ¼" with touching turns of thread at the thick end (where I always commence binding) to ensure that the splines would not move relative to one another, thereafter a ½" spiral of thread was steadily applied at a speed that allowed the excess glue to be extruded. Loops of thread were caught in at both ends from which a section could be suspended and tensioned and so kept straight by a weight of about 2lbs whilst the adhesive cured. The top section splines were bound in the same manner, though being thinner they had to be manipulated and treated rather more gently during the process to avoid introducing unwanted bends or kinks. The chances of this can be greatly reduced if some means of support can be contrived

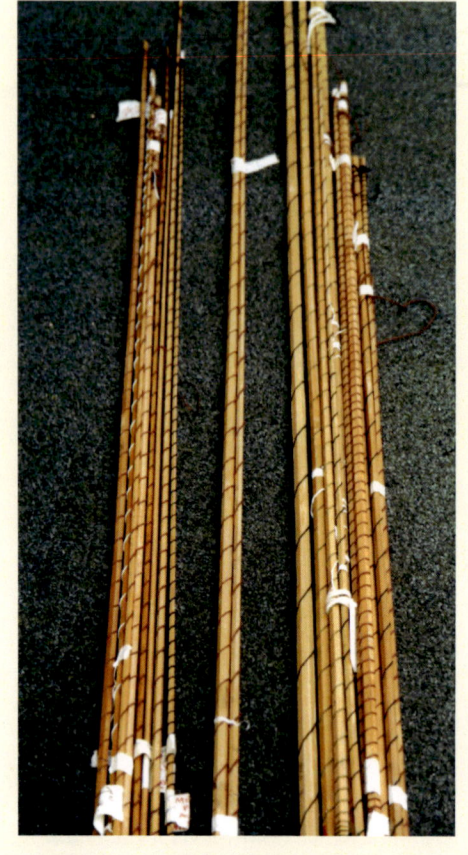

The gluing up process used for the rod shown in 1. (right) in the middle – 8'0" #5 2-piece. Various other completed splines will be done in due course, including a 10' carp rod

2. Splines in glue trough covered in adhesive

3. Arranging by numbers

4. Binding together

5. Rolling boards in use

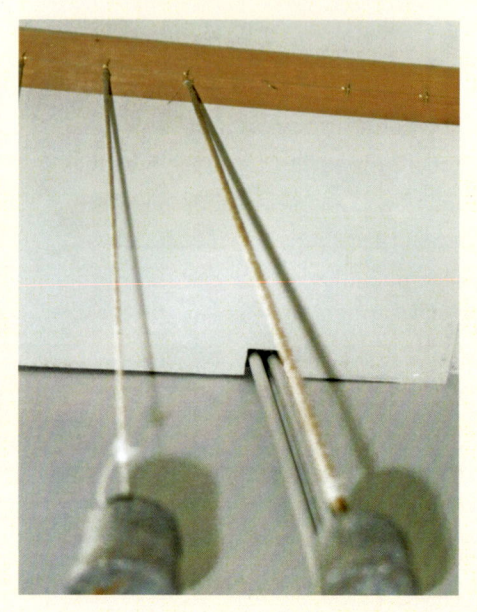

6. Hanging to cure in boiler room

48 | **The diary** | The diary of a rod

that allows the far end of the work to be supported as the 'near' end is being bound to stop it flopping about; 'rests' projecting from the bench to left and right are very useful in this respect (see photo 4, page 48).

Throughout the process a bowl of warm water was kept close by to keep my fingers clean and remove the stickiness. Cascamite does not irritate my skin but some other adhesives do: for example, when I use a resorcinol resin glue I wear a pair of thin latex rubber gloves which would probably also be wise in respect of any adhesive as even the chance of developing dermatitis is best avoided.

Both bound sections were rolled on the rolling boards to remove to as great a degree as possible any curves or bends that had been introduced and were inspected for any twists that might similarly have occurred which were eliminated by opposed twisting. It is worth taking some trouble over such 'faults' at this stage because they will be fixed during the curing process and so be much more difficult to eradicate. The elimination of twists is made much easier if a series of pencil dots is made along the outside face of one spline before glue is applied: they act as 'sighters' both during and after binding. Without them I find it hard sometimes to identify a twist in the finer parts of a top section – the eyes get dimmer as time passes! It is also advantageous if most of the excess squeezed out glue is wiped away. Do not do this with too wet a cloth which may dissolve and weaken the glue line along the section's edges.

The curing took place in the central heating boiler room where the temperature stays above 80°F constantly. Four or five hours will cure Cascamite at this temperature but I always leave the sections to cure far longer than this which is infinitely preferable to undercuring them. Indeed most modern adhesives do not achieve their full strength for several days (maybe as much as a week) after being cured for the requisite time at the recommended temperature. This has relevance relating to when a rod (or a bow) should be used in earnest if it is completed quickly after being bonded though of course it is perfectly acceptable to work on it before such a period has elapsed; such a consideration is not normally necessary in rod making as much has still to be done to produce a finished rod after the gluing.

Just as setting up the system took some time so did cleaning up 'the gear', a chore that cannot be forgotten if one has any intention of using it again so when all was complete I spent 30 minutes at this task even though uncured Cascamite is 'kind' and dissolves readily in hot soapy water. Session time *1¾ hours.*

Notes

Binding and adhesives

When I first made rods I bound the splines by what I called the 'foot trap method' which involved trapping the binding thread under my foot to tension it as I wound it on to the splines by hand. Dozens of rods were bound in this manner over a period of years and as far as I am aware none of them failed in the glue line and between them they have accounted for a very great number of fish so there cannot be anything too wrong with the process which is the simplest system I have ever employed.

The most sophisticated (if it may be so described) is the binder devised and employed by Garrison, my version of which was made from items that in the main I laid hands on in the workshop. I initially regarded this as a prototype but as it worked very well I have never made another. A photograph of it is shown opposite. The only things I can think of that I adopted in respect of this binder that are different from the usual are 1) a driving belt made of one continuous length of linen thread of about 7 lbs breaking strain with its two ends knotted together and then looped to make a three or four stranded belt in place of the more conventional spliced belt with a cross-sectional diameter of a little more than $1/16$". If a conventional type of belt is knotted (rather than spliced) the knot will surely jam as the device is operated but in the case of the multi-strand belt the knot is so small that it does not impede the action of the binder in the least. Indeed it will pass through the binder much more smoothly than the spliced driving belts I made. The making of the spliced belts took me back decades when bow strings of spliced linen thread were used in the days before the advent of Dacron and similar modern synthetic fibres, in fact I used bow string linen for the driving belts. And 2) the use of a fly reel with a drag system as a reservoir for and to tension the binding thread.

There is some leeway in respect of the pressure required for successful bonding which should be neither too little nor too great. If hand binding is undertaken the 'feel' of sufficient pressure can be established if a 1½ lb weight is suspended on a thread which can then be bound on to a piece of dowel so the tightness of the spiral (of thread) can be ascertained. Such a pressure is fine for trout sized rods; great crushing pressure is not required.

Two splices – one for a bow and one for a driving belt

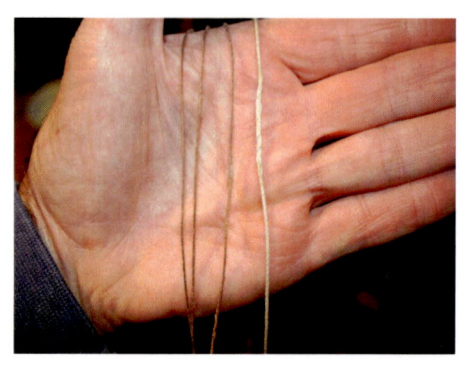

Two driving belts – one spliced and one multi-stranded

Just as I have tried various ways of binding the splines so over the years I have used a variety of good quality adhesives including Cascaphen (a resourcinol diluted with formaldehyde), an undiluted 'raw' resourcinol, two types of Aerolite in addition to the oft mentioned Cascamite

One Shot. All these are excellent for rod making but usually I opt for the last type because it is extremely convenient to use: one simply has to add water to create the glue, it is easy to apply, requires no special conditions for curing and the gear is easy to clean. It is also the cheapest of the options and its colour matches that of the bamboo so as to make good glue lines virtually indiscernible. Its bonding and waterproofing qualities are perfectly fine for rod making, indeed it can be used for small boat building for components above the waterline and it is a very durable product. Conversely raw resourcinol and Cascaphen, although having higher technical specifications than Cascamite, require higher curing temperatures of 100/110°F (38/40°C) if these properties are to materialise and thus probably some sort of custom-made hot box capable of reaching these temperatures is required. They also produce dark brown glue lines that are very visible and although not unsightly are a feature that I now tend to avoid though the dark lines do help when the bends are being removed from rod blanks as they act as clear sight lines. Epoxy resin glues (of which there seem to be endless varieties) I have used extensively for bow making where glass fibre laminates have to be bonded to wood cores but not for rod making; here again it is frequently necessary to cure these glues at high temperatures to develop their full adhesive potential and for this reason I have a large 'cupboard' type box heated with light bulbs. For those starting out on their rod making there are probably a number of good reasons for avoiding this type of adhesive which include its cost, relative to the other types, its 'touchiness' in respect of the moisture content of the components being bonded and the considerable difficulty of cleaning up afterwards (methylated spirits is a solvent for the uncured glue). It seems to me that there is a certain merit in operating with the most straightforward and 'simple to mix' adhesive that will do the job satisfactorily; simplicity allied with effectiveness are two qualities that seem to me to be very desirable in craft and probably all activities – certainly complexity for its own sake does not seem very appealing.

The old and the new

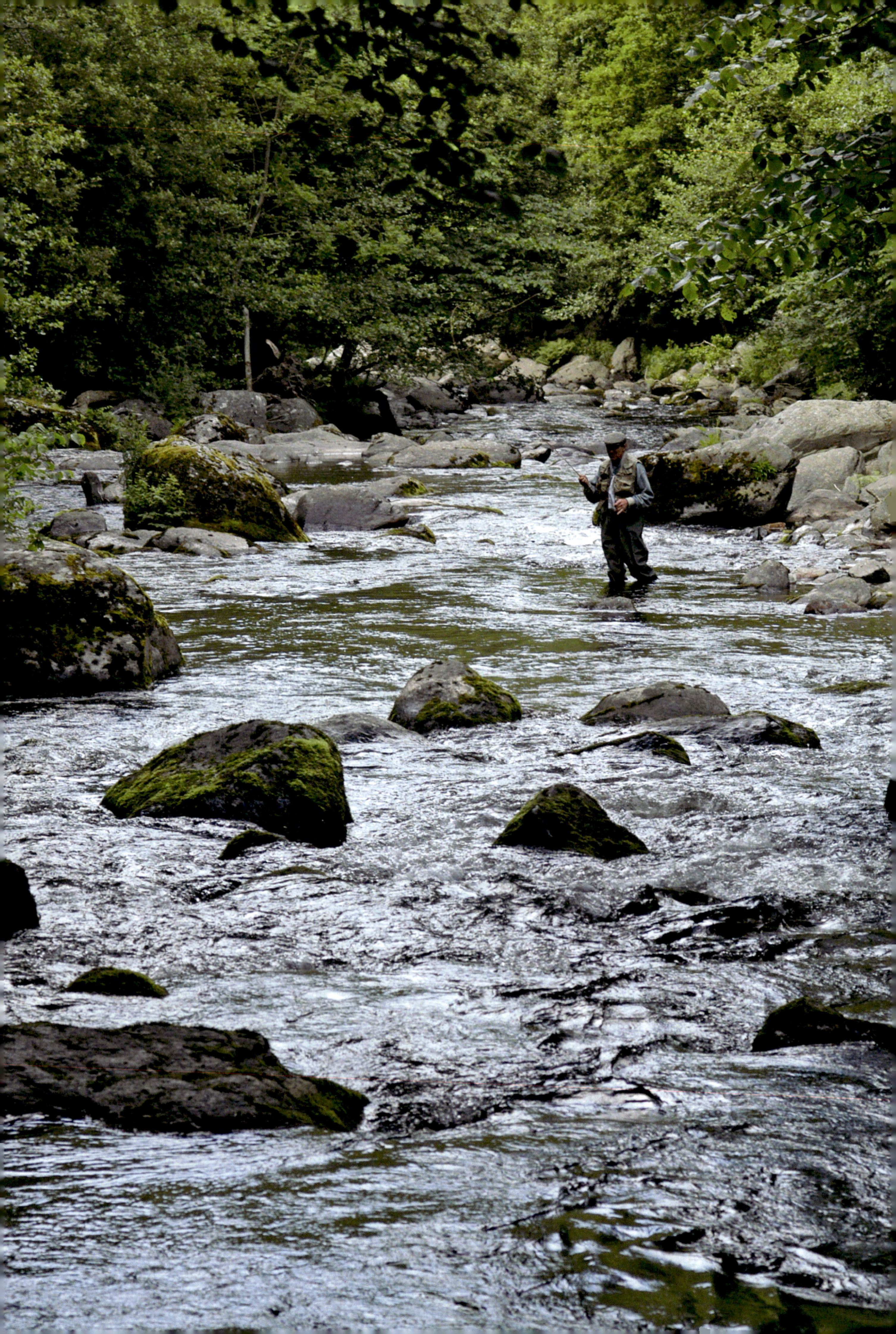

Session 12

Even after making many rods over a long period of time I still experience a frisson of excitement tinged with a little apprehension when it comes to removing the bindings from the newly bonded splines as after many hours of work the occasionally recalcitrant spindly lengths of bamboo will be in a recognisable (blank) rod form for the first time. If the gluing has gone well a rod will almost certainly result, if it has not then there is no chance of retrieving the situation and what was intended to be a rod will at best become lesser items such as ferrule stoppers, priest handles or some such things. Such childlike excitements are all part of the process and play their role in ensuring that rod making remains a captivating activity for which I am very thankful. Indeed when I first made rods I had to exercise great discipline in order to leave the sections strictly alone until the glue was fully cured despite knowing that only ruin would ensue if a partially cured blank was 'waggled' to see how it felt. I don't suffer now from the same degree of impatience which must be one of the very few advantages of getting older.

As the thread spiralled off the rod section it sent showers of glue in all directions which made the goggles I was wearing a necessary precaution as a sliver of glue in the eye is extremely irritating. Despite these shard like showers there was still some adhesive adhering to the surface which was eliminated with glass-paper wrapped around a cork block. This had to be done very carefully if the corners of the hexagon were not to removed and the surface power fibres damaged, particularly at the fine end of the top section. Initially just one face of the hexagon was carefully cleaned which made any twist and bend visually very obvious which in turn made the job of removing the twists, etc. rather easier.

Despite care having been taken when they were glued the rod sections did exhibit a few mild curves and a slight twist but no serious problems, i.e. sharp angles that can be extremely difficult and sometimes impossible to wholly remove. To neutralise these curves 18" portions of the blanks were heated in turn and subjected to 'contrary pressure' applied by hand and maintained until the bamboo was cool, the slight twist being removed in the same manner using the cleaned up surface mentioned above as a 'sighter'. Care had to be taken not to overheat the cane and cause the glue to break down, the amount of heat being judged by touch. The aim was for a temperature that did not require hand protection but felt quite hot when handled – not a very precise way of proceeding but one that works just fine unless you allow your attention to wander as you flourish the heat gun. The gun, on its low setting, provided the more gentle application of heat required for this process as compared with that needed for say curing the cane when its hottest mark was required. Wooden arrow steles can be straightened using exactly the same principle but in their case sufficient heat can be generated by simply rubbing them vigorously through the hands. With both parts of the rod straight and twist free the remaining five faces were cleaned off, a dusty job that required the use of the face mask, but after a while two very respectable rod sections lay on the work top.

When the straightening was done I had intended to fit the ferrules but somewhere along the line I sort of ran out of momentum and ground to a halt so I finished for the day, an indulgence that the professional cannot entertain. The session had lasted *1¾ hours*.

Notes

Straightness

Absolute straightness can be an elusive quality (even in carbon rods if they are viewed before they have rings put on them), however experience has taught me that very slight deviations will be 'lost' when the rings are whipped on and will not affect the rod's performance in any way that is detectable either cosmetically or in a practical sense. This is an important thought to keep in mind when starting out as a rod maker as it is in the early stages that such failings are likely to occur and when they are most likely to cause one the most concern. I seem to be blessed (or cursed) with an eye that is able to identify the minutest deviation from the straight, the vertical, the horizontal, etc. etc., which can be strangely disconcerting. For example, has anyone commented on the significant proportion of church steeples that are not quite vertical, nearly so but not quite?

So if a slight curve remains after all your best efforts to remove it don't despair. By placing the rings on its convex side everything will come nicely into line, particularly after a few fish have been landed as it is when it is in this mode that a rod is likely to suffer from taking a set. It is of course possible to purposely build mild curves into the blanks so that the rod after some use will not follow the 'string' (an archery term that is self-explanatory) but end up straight. Some thoughts on the use of cane rods can be found in the pages ahead that suggest some ploys that will go a long way to eliminating such dangers and prolonging the life of a rod at its full potential. I am not suggesting however that perfect straightness is not a desirable end – in all normal senses it is, but a natural material is being manipulated here in a form that will highlight the slightest of deviations (before ringing) and the rod maker has to work in harmony with the material to create the best product he can. Makers of wooden bows will understand this idea very well especially those who make bows from yew wood as they endeavour to 'release' the bow 'contained' in a stave. Their efforts may result in a weapon that does not match a theoretical norm in appearance but will nevertheless be an efficient and durable item. What is certain is that to subject a rod to extreme measures that might compromise its practical performance to achieve cosmetic perfection is not a wise thing to do. I have some rods in which I, as the maker, could point out some 'faults' that are still subduing fish twenty years after they were made and will continue to do so for many more if they are treated properly; in reality, over time, one forgets what the problem was or is.

I feel much the same way about the pursuit of very fine tolerances in diameter that are sometimes quoted in rod making publications, tolerances as little as ½ thou which, in the normal course of things, are hardly measurable. You only have to breathe on a piece of cane to make it swell that amount and we really are not making space shuttles here. Such tiny distinctions may sound very impressive but in reality they can act as inhibitors rather than encouragers to those who may feel the impulse to make a rod – it is better to press ahead within the scope of your expanding abilities, make a rod as well as you can, and go and catch a few fish with it. You will very quickly forget about its apparent dimensional inadequacies and anyway you can always determine to make one next time that does not exhibit these 'characteristics'. A rod does not have to be perfect to catch a lot of fish, at least those are my thoughts and maybe they are the best advice that this diary can offer.

Session 13

Fitting the ferrules is a job that I do not really enjoy as everyone (quite rightly) expects it to be done perfectly but is it also one that is remarkably easy to do just not quite right if one does not pay very close attention throughout the process. It is also a job that has serious implications in both a practical and an aesthetic sense so doing it well is doubly important.

Prior to fitting the ferrules the rod sections were reduced from 54" to 48" each which was done by removing 3" from both ends of each section; when the splines were planed to their final size I arranged that the removal of these amounts of material would leave diameters of the proper size.

A pair of bronze splint ended ferrules were selected that required the bamboo to be reduced to achieve a good fit, which is standard practice provided, and it is a big provided, NO material is removed from the cane beyond a point about halfway along the splint ends. The same principle pertains when the horn nocks are fitted to the tips of a traditional long bow, except in this case the holes in the nocks are tapered as must be the tips of the bow. With this important rule well to the front of my mind along with the thought of how easily a crooked fit could be created the bamboo was carefully and symmetrically reduced with a medium grade file and glass-paper. It was tested many times for a good fit by being pushed into the ferrule and rotated whereupon the high spots would reveal themselves as dark friction marks, which would indicate where further reduction was required. As long as the cane remained oversized and in line all was well but as the difference between oversize and a loose fit can be just a few strokes of the file the reduction proceeded slowly to the point were both portions of the ferrule slid smoothly to the required amount on to their respective parts of the rod. When this was achieved the splint ends of the ferrules were tapered with a fine grade file (though not when they were in position on the cane) to allow the bindings to flow evenly, without gaps, over the junction of metal and cane. After this they were mounted on the rod and the tapered splint portions were 'worked on', i.e. rolled under a piece of flat hard wood – ebony in this case – to make them assume its hexagonal shape, and before the conservationists amongst you gasp in horror I have had the ebony for about 40 years, well before much thought was given to the demise of the rain forests.

Strong nylon thread was used to temporarily bind the ferrules in place so the rod could be assembled and checked for straightness as the tiniest deviation (surprise surprise!) from a straight fit can put what seems an amazing angle in a rod. Fortunately these ferrules did not suffer from this malady so I could proceed straightaway with permanently fixing them with a fast setting epoxy resin but not before a tiny hole had been drilled in the end of the male to allow trapped air to escape as the ferrule was being pushed on to the rod. Without this little hole a ferrule is quite capable of sliding slyly out of position if the fit is very good since the adhesive acts as a seal to compress the air trapped in the tube as the ferrule is pushed into position which of course expands again as soon as the pressure is released and before the temporary bindings can be secured – crafty blighters ferrules unless you keep a close eye on them!

Although I 'only' fitted the ferrules today it still took me *1 hour*. It would of course have been done much quicker with a lathe though I suppose it does illustrate that ferrules can be fitted by hand even if it is a rather protracted job.

Cane carefully reduced to fit in ferrule – parallel fit

Small hole to release trapped air

Splint end bound down during gluing

Sometimes a butt will have to be built up with veneers to enable a proper fit to be acheived even though the tip has to be reduced as shown above

Horn nocks for string on long bows – tapered fit

Notes

Cutting sections to length and ferrule dressing

There is no absolute need to initially make rod sections as much longer as was done with these, though it is quite normal to have an extra inch or so of length. The reason that I favour this system is because I have always found that it is easier to create a good straight section if the end portions are discarded, particularly if they have had suspension loops bound on to them (as they usually do) as these can put a kink in the bamboo which is not always easy to eliminate. The idea of making a longer than required section came from hand making arrows where it is hard to produce a high quality item if one works on a batten of the same length as the required finished arrow as it is difficult to make the very ends of the dowel to the same standard of roundness since the rest. For example, if a 28" arrow of say 5/16" diameter is required then it is best to start with say a 34" long batten 3/8" square and block plane and glass-paper it round and then discard the ends which will produce a shaft that is very true (round) to its very ends; I apply the same principle to rod sections.

When a pair of ferrules are purchased the two parts must be checked for general workmanship, fit which should be smooth and 'even' and for the two parts to engage wholly with one another. The fault I have mostly encountered is that of the male portion being marginally too large; rarely does one seem to come across a loose fit.

Reducing an oversized male ferrule has to be done with care, employing extremely fine wet or dry abrasive paper or cloth. My preferred method of proceeding is to mount and secure the ferrule on a suitably sized (short) length of dowel and spin it in the electric drill or a lathe, apply the cloth gently and constantly keep testing for size but only when the abrasive residue has been thoroughly wiped from the ferrule as it is really not a good idea to gum up the joint with this waste material. If this system is not to your liking then it can be done by hand though this is a much slower affair; sometimes abrasive paper is not required and the job can be accomplished using a metal polish such as Brasso. Just as when the bamboo was being reduced to fit into the ferrules every care must be taken not to make a loose fit as this will create a problem that is harder to rectify than the original one: some method has then to be employed to compress the female tube in a concentric manner, which usually involves the use of a substantial three (or more) jawed chuck normally used with a metal working lathe; you do not need the lathe but you do need the chuck and a chuck key. In my experience the chucks normally used with a hand electric or pillar drill are not robust enough for the job which sometimes requires considerable force to 'compress' an oversized female ferrule, force that has to be applied with great restraint if a sudden collapse is to be avoided. In a later section some ideas are put forward which make the use of ferrules redundant.

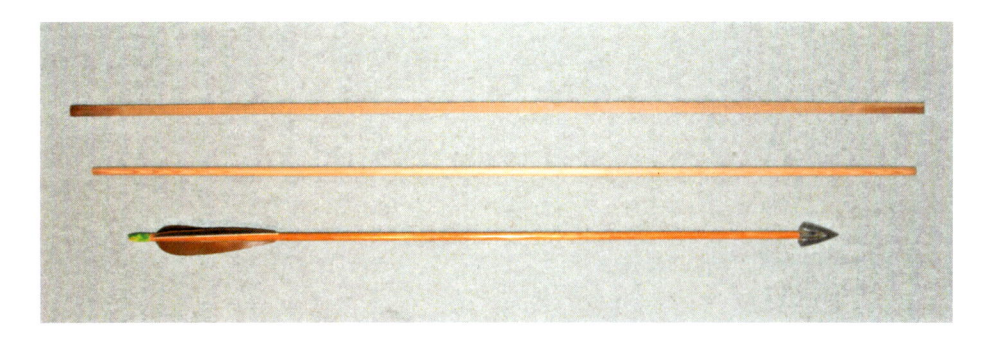

A 34" batten turns into a 28" hunting arrow

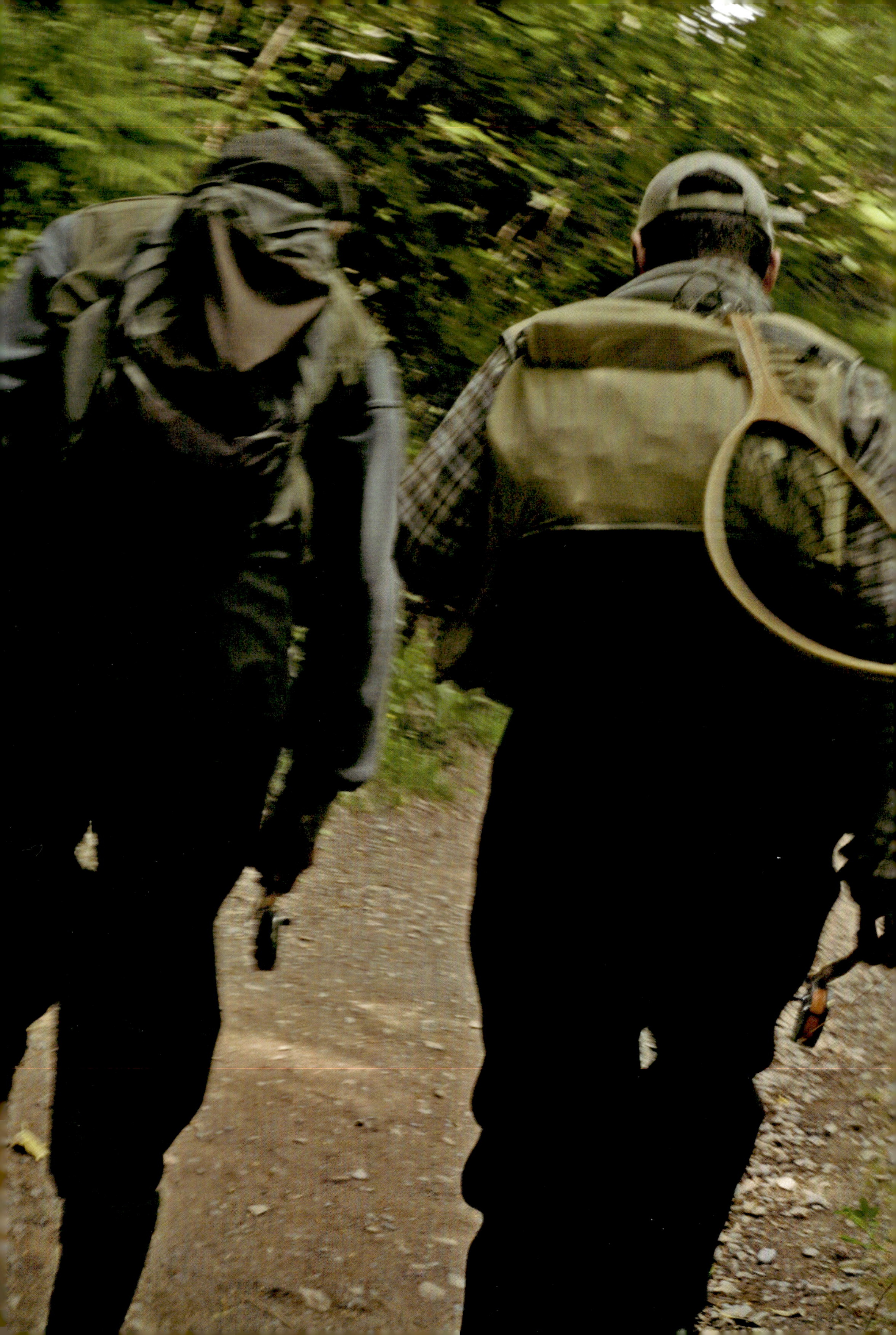

Session 14

The first job today was to remove the temporary ferrule bindings and clean off the squeezed-out epoxy using a sharp blade followed by abrasive paper, a job requiring a careful touch if the cane was to remain undamaged where it emerged from under the ferrule splints. This was accomplished without mishap and the rough temporary bindings were replaced with neatly applied ones which extended on to the cane for about ⅝" after which I could not resist assembling the rod and giving it a wiggle. Such wiggling is no acid test of a rod's potential but it felt OK which was pleasing despite the fact that numerous rods of the same dimensions had been made previously.

Before being stored in a warm, dry place the blanks were smoothed with fine glass-paper before being 'polished' with extremely fine 'second hand' flour paper, i.e. it had had its sharpness removed so that it buffed rather than abraded the surface of the bamboo. Also the sharp angles of the hexagonal section were marginally dulled in the belief that this would allow the protective finish to adhere more positively along the edges and so resist rather better any tendency to being chipped off. By marginally I mean that each corner received a couple of passes of flour paper along its length which in reality means that I probably need hardly have bothered but it made me feel that heed was being paid to the principle of good adhesion which sometimes is not so good along a fine edge.

CORK (SHRIVES) GLUED INTO PLACE ON MANDRILS IN READINESS FOR BEING SHAPED INTO REEL SEATS

... AND HANDLES WITH RASPS, FILES AND ABRASIVE PAPERS

The second part of the session was taken up with shaping the cork handle and reel seat from shrives that had been glued together the previous evening with Cascamite on steel mandrills – 13 for the handle and 6 for the reel seat for the size of shrives that were available – a task that took about 20 minutes. The job was done by hand after the grip of the adhesive on the mandrill had been broken by giving the mandrill a sharp tap when it was positioned in a hole in the bench that acted as a stop for the corks which, at this stage, were still full size. By holding and rotating the mandrill in one hand and continually observing the work the cork was rasped, filed and glass-papered into shape before being spun in an electric drill to achieve a smooth finish. When working in this way the trick seems to be to allow the weight of the tools rather than the strength of one's arms to do the work – a comment that has already been made in relation to some other procedure I think – too much force just breaks up the cork. Particular care had to be taken with the reel seat which was initially pared down in a concentric fashion in relation to its mandrill with a very keen, thin-bladed knife to ensure that the correct relationship was achieved between its diameter and that of the sliding rings that will secure the reel. Get this wrong 'on the small side' and another seat will have to be made.

The sliding rings were cut from a length of knurled aluminium pipe, portions of which can be sawn off as required, bevelled on one inside edge with a sharp knife so that they easily slip over the lip of the reel flange and generally smoothed so as not to present any sharp edges when in use. The holes in the handle and seat were adjusted with a round rasp to fit on to the cane, though fitting will not happen until the rod has received its protective coating which is a job that will be done shortly. A *1¾ **hour*** session which includes the 20 minutes work of the previous evening.

A TIGHT FIT IS PREFERABLE TO A LOOSE ONE AS IT IS FIXABLE WHEREAS THE OTHER IS NOT. AT LEAST NOT AS EASILY

SLIDING RINGS ON DEMAND

Notes

Corks

The cork shrives were of standard quality. I have never been tempted to use the top fluor grade stuff which doubtless would be good to work with but has the disadvantage of being literally almost worth its weight in gold and after a few months' hard wear and tear might not look any better than the ordinary quality – at least that's how I convince myself that I am not mean, just thrifty!

Sometimes just for fun a champagne cork will be incorporated into the handle or reel seat of a rod – Veuve Cliquot or Bollinger of course! No, only joking! It is far more likely to be a Tesco's or Sainsbury's special offer as I don't operate in Cliquot circles (more's the pity) though some Moet et Chandon and Lanson corks that have been used for this purpose must have come from quite grand affairs but I cannot remember where, which might be a comment in itself! These corks saved from, say, a wedding or an anniversary or some such happy event and then used in this way act as a more or less permanent reminder of those happy times – one rod was named 'The 7-7-77' after a wedding that happened on that date, the handle of which incorporated an appropriate cork – foolishness an amateur can indulge in without penalty and if friends do comment on the odd looking end to their reel seat they never do so to the point of refusing a rod which is usually a gift.

Even when I have a lathe available I do not stick shrives on to the rod blanks and shape the handle in situ as I have a great fear that the blank may somehow loosen in the lathe and then be thrashed to splinters before it can be stopped. The fear however is not unfounded as I have seen woodworking lathes do some amazing things to the items that were meant to be turned on them – for example, hurling a partially turned large bowl across a workshop of considerable size, up the opposite wall and part way back along the ceiling, which cleared the room as quickly as anything one could imagine.

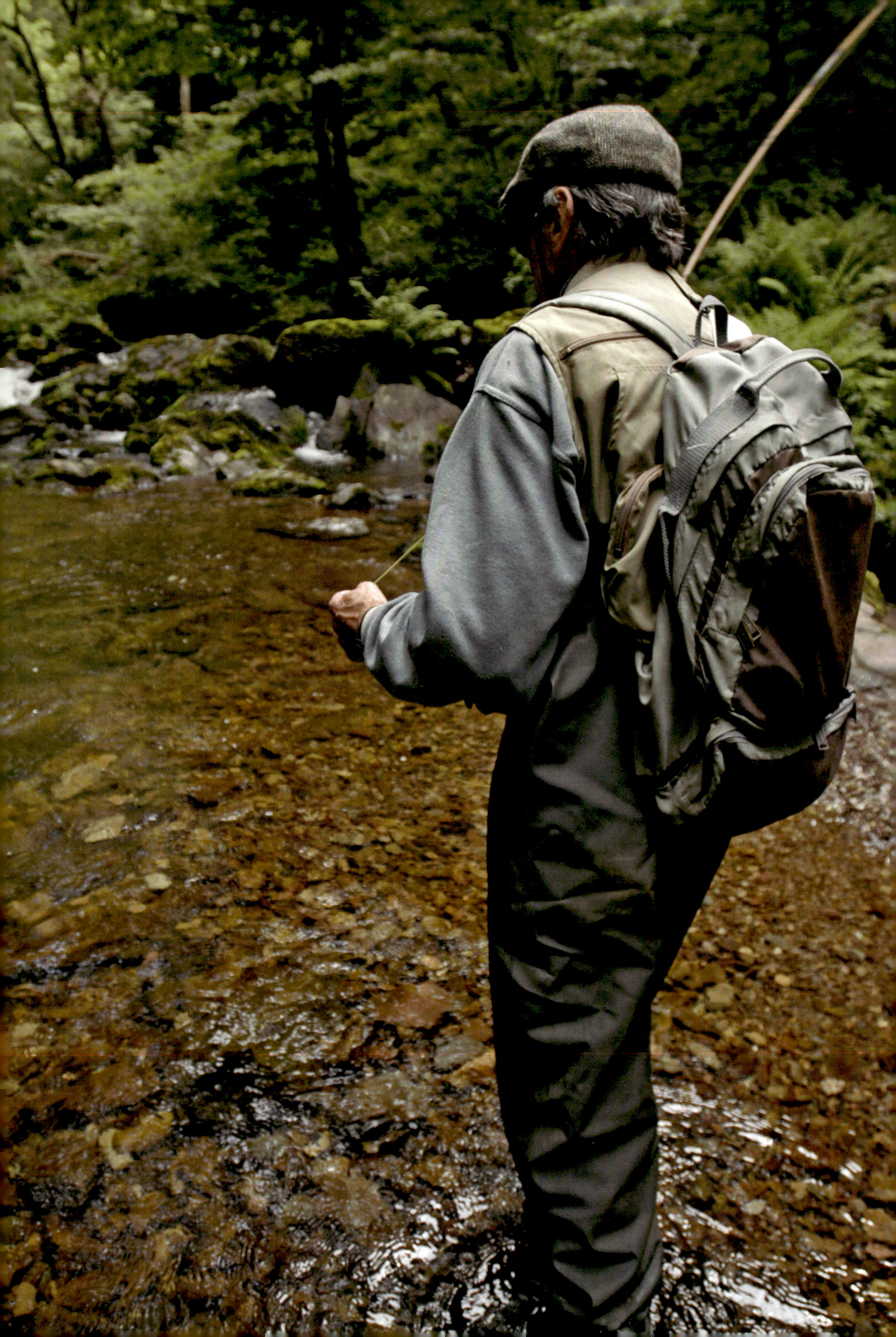

Session 15

At this point the route to completing the rod can take one of two paths: either the rings can be put on or the sections can receive the first coat of protective finish. Both of these have been tried at various times and although there are some implications in respect of which is chosen these are not really significant enough to make one route obviously the better choice. For example, if the sections are dipped first then some time must be allowed to elapse before the ringing takes place to enable the finish to cure thoroughly, which usually takes a few days or else its surface may be marred, whereas ringing a rod first requires more care when the sections are withdrawn from the dip tank and requires the subsequent removal of varnish from the rod rings.

Today I took the route of putting on the rings, the first part of which operation was to mark their positions with spacings as shown in the diagram. Ten rings, or guides if you prefer, were put on made up of a hard chrome loop tip, eight snakes of graduated size and a hard lined butt or stripper ring which seems about correct for a rod of this length. If fewer are used there is the danger that the line will not be sufficiently controlled and may generally slap about reducing the chances of good control and presentation whilst too many will unnecessarily encumber the rod and 'weigh' it down and possibly detract from its performance and involve small needless expense.

Once the spacings had been established one foot of each ring was secured with masking tape to allow the other to be bound firmly in place. This is something that is very easy to do now that the feet of the snake rings come ready tapered allowing a neat gapless binding to be achieved particularly if the thread is wound 'up the slope' from cane to ring so that each turn of thread supports the succeeding one. The loose end of the thread is finally drawn back under the last few securing turns by means of a loop in the standard fashion. Formerly snake feet (!) had to be tapered on a grindstone which was a job I loathed for no wholly explicable reason except that I did. The ready tapered variety are therefore greatly appreciated. The stalky ends of the secured tying thread were carefully removed with a very sharp blade so as not to leave any wisps of material which would mar the appearance of the finished rod. The thread being brown in colour and of a moderately fine sort – Grade A Gudebrod – which matches the physical dimensions of the rod and the rings. You may wonder why the reel seat and handle were not also put on at this stage, the answer to which is twofold: 1) by dipping all the cane of the butt section one can be sure that dampness cannot do its mischief unseen under the cork and 2) it allows the ferrule to be kept clear of the finish and so removes the necessity of plugging up its hole and then of cleaning it off, neither of which are great chores but can be avoided by working in this way.

The rings were put on in a casual sort of way over the course of an evening whilst a bit of television was watched and by the time the tip ring had been glued in place with some quick set epoxy about *1½ hours* had elapsed and the rod was ready to receive its protective coating.

Notes

Intermediate bindings

With the advent of modern adhesives the need to add intermediate bindings has become redundant though some rods still sport them for cosmetic reasons as they create a traditional appearance that is favoured by some users. As far as I am concerned they are something of a nuisance as they take me far longer to apply than the rings and are another of those jobs that it is easier to do poorly than perfectly so unless there is a very pressing reason for adding them (like having my arm thoroughly twisted) the rods in the main do without the 'traditional' look. It is not just a case of the fiddly nature of the task in which the bindings should become progressively closer together as the rod tip is approached but because of the difficulty in securing tightly a binding of just two or three turns of thread before they just 'fall off' the rod. I have only two rods decorated in this fashion which were done out of curiosity which was very quickly satisfied I am afraid to say.

If a shoulder collar is used to mask the junction of cane and cork then some thought needs to be given as to when it is added to the rod if the handle is to be put on after dipping as was done in this instance – no rocket science is required but it is usually not possible to push it into position from the butt end particularly if the butt has any degree of swell.

Session 16

This session saw the rod receive its first coat of protective finish of high grade polyurethane applied by means of a dipping tank, if a piece of 1½ d. clear acrylic tubing stopped at one end can be graced with such a title. The 54" tube was filled to within a few inches of the top to allow for the increase in depth occasioned by the immersion of the rod and was then allowed to stand for a while so that all the little bubbles caused by pouring in the finish could come to the surface and be dispersed with the aid of a little brush.

Before the sections were dipped they were wiped down with acetone for the same reasons as the splines were before gluing. Once immersed the sections were withdrawn with the aid of an old fly reel cranked by hand and not the more usual method of a slowly rotating motor. My reasons for this are that I am loath to leave the emerging sections to their own devices as on my return some of the little bubbles just dispersed may have reinvented themselves and stuck on the bamboo from where they can sometimes be frustratingly difficult to remove. Similarly I am usually unminded to do any work that might create a dust and as I make relatively few rods in the great scheme of things I see a motor as no great advantage. As it happens, these sections had to be dipped in the house as that is the only place where I have sufficient headroom to allow the 48" rod sections to clear the top of the 54" dipping tube; the 9'0" ceiling height allows this to happen with a few inches to spare; shorter lengths can be accommodated in the workshop.

Each section took about 12 minutes of quiet work to withdraw with the fine artist's brush kept at the ready to remove any bubbles that happened to appear. After this they were taken to a warm still-aired room so that the surface had the best chance of remaining blemish free. Despite the fact that dipping requires more of a 'set-up' than the straightforward brushing on of the 'varnish' that was the method I used in the past, the results it achieves particularly in cosmetic terms are so much better that the extra input involved is more than worthwhile.

The session lasted *1 hour* when the setting up and clearing up times were added to that of the dipping. As the next coating was to be applied in a day or so the dipping tube was not emptied of finish but simply well sealed and left to stand.

Here I am breaking from the pattern of this diary by not giving the second dipping a session of its own but as it was the same as the first apart from the clearing up it seemed rather unnecessary to reiterate what has already been recorded. The unused finish was poured back into its tin where I find it lasts much better than when left for a long period in the tube and the gear was thoroughly cleaned with white spirit. I shall however add the *1½ hours* it took to the total of hours worked when the final reckoning is done.

Notes

Various finishes and thoughts on their application

Bamboo can be successfully protected with a variety of finishes that are readily available and relevant (in terms of application) to the small-scale rod maker. Over the years I have tried a number of different formulations including one and two part cellulose systems, spar varnishes, tung oil type mixtures and polyurethane, all of which will harden well on cane unlike some tropical hardwoods which are inimical to spirit-based finishes. I have no experience of the surface impregnation process that some manufactured rods and such things as wooden kitchen-ware (knife handles) undergo. I suspect however that a hobbyist could set himself up to do so if he wished, depending on just how involved with caustic soda and pressure baths of phenolic resin he wants to become.

There are a number of things that are worth considering before dipping: for example, if a large diameter dipping tank is used then it will take a big volume of expensive finish to fill it so it is best to do some experimenting with tubes of various diameters and water before making a decision even if you intend to have a system that enables a vacuum to be formed in the tank when it is not in use and so prolong the life of the finish. A 1½"d. pipe 54" long will hold about 2 litres of finish that will not last indefinitely despite being of sufficient volume to protect dozens of rods. Because my 'tank' (tube!) is so rudimentary I have found it convenient to have a selection of different lengths to match the length of the rod that I happen to be dipping; to fill a 54" tube when say a 4-piece 7'0" rod is being dipped seems pointless if only because cleaning out the shorter tube is easier (see later chapter concerning such multipiece rods). The question of adequate headroom has already been touched on, but if you are not allowed to play in the house for whatever reason then a short tube that enables just more than one half of a (long) section to be dipped can be utilised. One half of the section is dipped and allowed to dry before the other is similarly treated in a subsequent operation. To avoid a 'tide mark' where the two coats meet the section can be dipped to a point that will coincide with a binding for a rod ring. At a stroke the necessity for a high-ceilinged space and a large volume of liquid are done away with.

When dipping a section that has previously had its rings bound on it is necessary to stop the withdrawal process for a moment just after a ring has emerged to allow the liquid dammed up by the ring to flow evenly back into the reservoir and not cause unsightly runs on the surface. This is another reason that I do not use an automatic system as the on/off switch would require resetting each time a rod with different ring spacings was dipped. When manually withdrawn there is no absolute necessity for the section to emerge at a constant rate throughout the process – I find that say 3–4" can be slowly cranked out followed by a pause without the quality of the final finish being compromised in any way.

The viscosity of the finish (and the working temperature) has implications for the speed of withdrawal: a very viscous one will require a slower speed to allow the 'the flow back' to occur in a proper manner as the thicker liquid simply will not travel over the surface as quickly as a thin one. The polyurethanes that are now available remain fluid even at quite cold temperatures, which is a great help during the colder months, but even so I am sure that it is best to apply and cure them in pleasant warm, dry conditions.

Usually the rods I make do not receive multiple layers of finish, as after a certain point they add little by way of extra protection and just thicken and dull off the rod's action. When discussing the things that are added to the bamboo and can affect its potential with some aircraft engineering friends I was surprised at the especial attention they paid to the thickness and thus the weight of varnish and its effect on a rod's performance, in which they appeared more interested than the more apparently obvious 'heavy' (to the layman) items such as rod rings and ferrules. When they really got into their stride and started considering vortex shedding, with me nodding more in panic than understanding, it did cross my mind that the only thing that was likely to fly on this rod would be a BWO or a PT nymph and would they know the difference? We were not designing a jet fighter here and maybe one can know too much about something in certain circumstances. Anyway, taking my cue from all this I have for ages applied only two coats to the rods which has in no way I can detect exposed them to greater risk than the rods that formerly received maybe three or even four layers of finish; I guess however that in the end it's a question of what one feels happy with.

Wet varnish makes very good fly paper but this is best avoided for both rod finish and fly

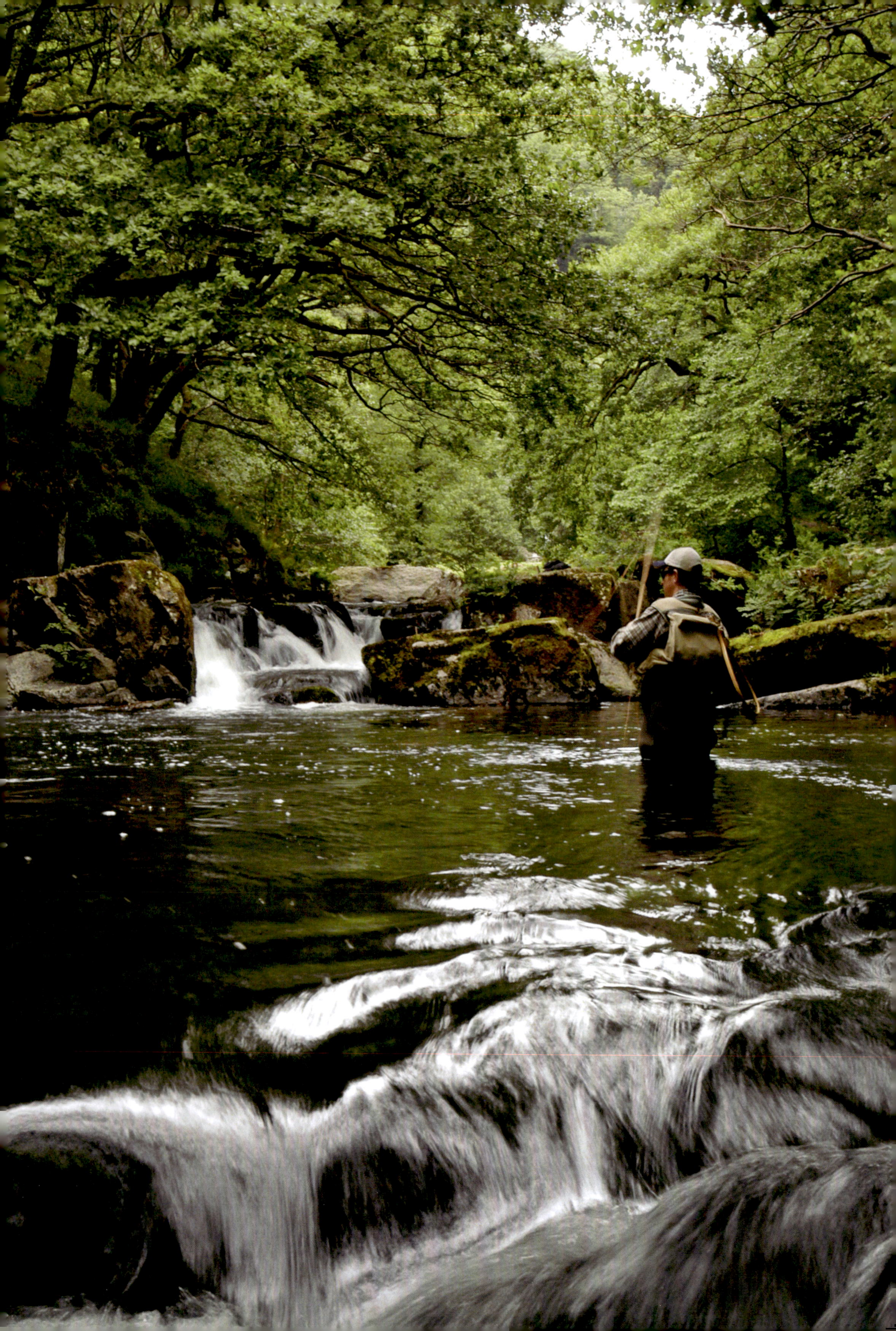

Session 17

The handle and reel seat were glued in position today with rapid-set epoxy and the 'shoulder' and keeper ring whippings added before the 'ink work' was done, by which I mean the information that is found written either in long hand or is printed on the butts of most rods. The kit for this job is very basic and consists of a bottle of Indian ink, an old-fashioned dip pen, a damp rag for erasing any errors, a small, soft sable brush and a small quantity of polyurethane finish to protect the wording, and to seal the bindings mentioned above. Indian ink will chip off a glazed surface very easily unless covered by a couple of coats of protective 'varnish'.

Finally just a word about the sliding rings that secure the reel: do not forget to put them on the reel seat with the correct orientation before you glue it into position. I would prefer not to be questioned too closely why this pearl of wisdom is offered! What was it that Forrest Gump said 'just happens'?

A ferrule stopper, made from a spare length of built cane, was also 'inked' to identify which rod it is to protect. By this time the session had lasted about 1¼ **hours.** The rod is now complete apart from the addition in a day or so of the second layer of varnish over the ink which will be a five-minute job after which it will be 'rested' to allow everything to cure and harden thoroughly before being 'dry' tested on The Green behind the house.

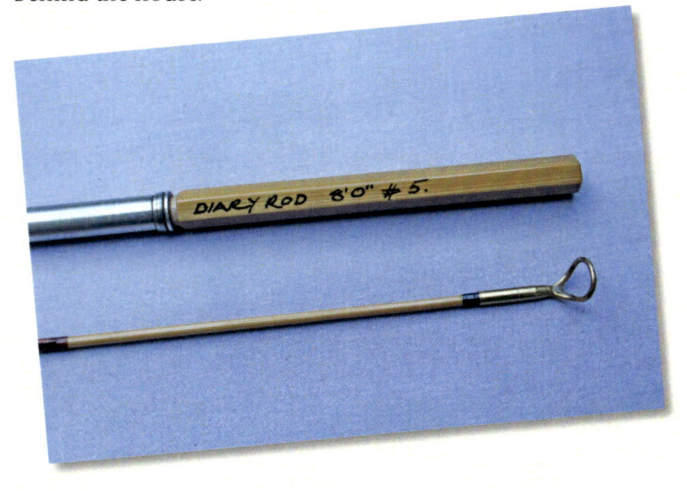

All set to go for the lettering

Notes

Details of information added to rod

The information that was put on was fairly standard and was as follows – rod length, line size, date it was made, maker's name (me) and the rod's title which in this case was 'Diary Rod' for which there will be no prizes for being able to guess why! Over the years rods have been given a variety of names – 'Hill Stream', 'Sea Trout', 'Grayling', 'Brylleth', 'Sewin', etc., being some that come quickly to mind which describe the place or the type of fish I had in mind when the rods were being built. Sometimes however a rod will be given a name that has little or nothing to do with fly fishing: for example, a few rods have been christened 'Champagne Rod' because a cork from that sort of wine was incorporated in their reel seats – (see Session 14 and the accompanying photographs). It was of course presumptuous to think that their performance might merit their title but as those who received them as gifts or near gifts seemed more than pleased with them I let the name stand.

One 'non standard' feature that is very convenient to have on a rod is a measuring scale that will allow the speedy release of any fish that warrants having its statistics recorded. If such a scale is added then it is most conveniently placed on the face of the hexagon that is opposite to the one on which the rod rings are bound as it is this face which will most readily present itself due to the counterbalancing position of the reel as a fish is offered up for measuring.

If a replacement butt has to be made for a damaged rod then it is a nice touch if a facsimile of the original lettering can be reproduced, which is possible if a bit of practice is conducted with the lettering pen even if initially one does not find this sort of thing comes naturally. The effort is worth it as the recipient of the handiwork is invariably pleased to have the 'old' rod back, so to speak. Adding really copperplate ink work almost certainly requires a steadier hand than mine though I hasten to add this is not because of the availability of the champagne corks used in reel seats. Generally it is possible to make things at least half decent with a bit of practice.

A rod 'scale' makes measurement a very quick affair

Conclusion to the diary

I have never before monitored the making of a rod so closely and will probably never do so again though the exercise turned out to be interesting and informative and I learned precisely some things that I previously knew only in a general sense. For example, if my addition is correct it took 25 hours and 35 minutes so let's say 25 hours of actual working time, proceeding in my usual and sometimes haphazard manner, to complete the project. I have no idea how long other amateur rod makers of some years' experience take to convert a culm into a rod but 25/30 hours is probably near the mark if they do not involve themselves in making a second top or say ferrules and winch fittings. If they have the facilities for such metal work they will require a few extra hours or may indeed become too engrossed in the minutiae of each step of the process and so could prolong the project endlessly. Although the amateur need not be at all as conscious as the professional in respect of the time spent at the bench to aim however to make a rod within a time scale that prevents the whole enterprise from becoming stale and maybe even boring is a good thing I am sure; 25/30 hours should avoid the onset of ennui.

At this stage the rod appears fine without any obvious defects and my feeling is that the project has been successful, but of course its true quality or lack of it will only become apparent when it has been used for an amount of time on the water. Sometimes well made and cosmetically beautiful looking rods do not perform as well as their appearance might lead one to suppose they should – it's not that they are bad rods it's just that they seem to lack that certain spark that separates the good from the average or indeed the excellent from the good. The next chapter examines this rod's performance and ways in which its performance can be sustained over time.

Although the rod just described is conventionally joined with a metal ferrule, 'Diary Rods' with spliced joints have also been made, as can be seen in a succeeding chapter

CANE OR CARBON, SAGE OR STRANG

No, I have not developed delusions of grandeur in linking my name with that of a foremost rod maker but I liked the cadence in the words of the title which pose a question that has already been answered by the tens of thousands of fly fishers who use carbon not cane. However a case can be made for those who occasionally or habitually use cane rather than its synthetic counterpart that suggests they are not wholly without reason.

The late Richard Walker wrote to me many years ago saying that bamboo rods were excellent for use on small to medium sized rivers, thoughts that are still valid today where the casting distance required is modest and the weight of the natural material remains manageably small as is the case with rods up to 8'0" (4ozs for the Diary Rod against say 1½-2 for a comparable carbon). The weight differential may be great at 50% or more but in absolute terms is likely to be insignificant to all but the markedly physically disadvantaged or weak. Once the slower more deliberate action of bamboo has been accommodated in one's casting style and attention paid to its greater capacity for being over stressed by unimaginative use then it should enrich and enlarge a fly fisher's experience base.

More contentious is the suggestion of using cane on larger waters, particularly still waters, where longer casting is almost invariably required which in turn demands a longer rod which will be significantly heavier in an absolute way than its modern equivalent. However the idea need not be dismissed out of hand if thought is given to the reel (very light composites are now available) and care is exercised in the choice of line which ideally should be weight forward with as fine a running line as possible, which may require that it be self made. I have just conducted some tests on The Green behind the house with two rods, one cane and one carbon, both 9'4" #7s which weigh 12ozs and 8ozs respectively with the reels in place. Ten casts were made with each rod, the longest and shortest of which were discarded and the remainder averaged, with results as follows - Carbon 32yds and Cane 27yds, which illustrate at least two things: 1) I am clearly not the world's greatest distance caster and 2) a bamboo rod will cast a perfectly fishable distance. These casts will seem, indeed are, very modest when set against the huge distances tournament casters achieve. However, I learned long ago that for ordinary mortals many imagined 40 yard throws diminish considerably when a tape measure is produced. Similarly many 'certain' 2lb river trout or grayling only move the needle to the 1¾lb mark if one is foolish enough to weigh them though I suspect that weight watchers may have a different opinion about scales! Indeed I accepted long ago that if I wish to make prodigious casts or catch weighty fish both the tape and the scales had better be left behind.

Anyway back to rods. Just as the reel and line need to be thought about so do the time, place and mode of fishing if the limitations of these large cane rods are to be minimised. For example, on still waters trout are quite prone to come close in as the light fades. I have sometimes waded out at this time only to find fish rising behind me when it has become a question of not how far can I cast but how short - so much for reaching the horizon! Slow retrieve nymphing reduces the number of casts in a session and boat fishing the distance required, both of which partly neutralise the greater rod weight which is most enervating when casting frequently and/or far.

Finishing where I started, of course carbon rods will remain predominant as they are such excellent tools, but just as a wooden hunting bow will do what is required of it so will a bamboo rod but in a more measured way than their synthetic counterparts.

Testing and care of your rod

'Caught anything yet?' is a question that I have been asked any number of times over the past thirty years or so as a new rod has been introduced to a line on The Green behind the house. At first this put me on the back foot but I soon learned to reply in kind, 'No, not yet but I didn't catch them all yesterday so I am still hopeful!' which usually brings the conversation to a close though I am sure that many walk off thinking 'What a daft bloke' but that is their problem. The most sensible question came from some children who asked 'Are you practising for a competition?' to which my response was I hope as sensible as their inquiry; certainly they fully accepted that trying out a new toy was a perfectly understandable activity.

However well one believes a rod has been made (or indeed *has* been made) it is not until it is used for some time in its operating environment that its true worth can be really established. Though not as relevant as the real thing 'dry testing' will give a pretty good idea of how a rod will perform as a casting tool especially if the line is lubricated from a bucket of water – in which some observers on The Green expect to see some fish I am sure! So what can be said about this rod? Well, it worked well when between about 7 and 12 yards of #5 line were aerialised, with the best response being achieved when about 10/11 yards of line were in the air. It would put out 15 or 16 yards without apparent complaint though rarely if ever will it be required to make these long throws on the rivers I fish. This was satisfying as I had hoped that it would not be too 'line specific', i.e. require a very precise amount of line to get it to function in anything like a satisfactory fashion. Clearly all rods have an optimum length of line that they favour but one that is versatile and forgiving in this respect is very desirable as it allows for its use in a variety of locations, i.e. 'tight' little streams as well as larger more open waters. As line was lengthened the action could be felt progressively farther down the butt section pretty much to where it disappeared under the corks but not into the handle to any degree which might have left the impression of a rod lacking in backbone. I was happy with this because it meant that when fully loaded all the rod above the handle was taking its share of the load but still left one with the sense of casting from a solid base.

In the first season I kept a close record of its use and performance on various waters which shows that it was used on 20 occasions on rivers of medium size where the fish were in the main in its 'weight category'; between May and December it accounted for 72 trout, 169 grayling with a few perch and chub thrown in for good measure making a grand total of 246 fish. None of the fish were exceptional, the largest trout being 1¼ lbs and the biggest grayling 1½, and most were less than 1¼ lbs and 1lb respectively. All this fishing was done with a good quality DT #5 line (Cortland) with tippets that did not normally exceed 3lbs. The exception was if a weighted shrimp or bug pattern was employed to plumb the depths when a heavier leader would facilitate turnover and its thicker diameter would prove no handicap in getting the fish to accept the offering as they seem to be less wary when a fly is deep down in their domain. At 8'0" it suited me best for fly presentation on or in the upper layers of water – dry fly, emerger patterns and sub surface nymph. For deeply presented flies such as shrimp and grub patterns I prefer a rather longer rod. However on a number of occasions it accounted for fish on all four methods – dry, emerger, sunk nymph and grub – which made those sessions quite memorable. The fish were all caught with upstream casting which is the style of fishing I favour and because the rules of the waters usually demanded it with the fly being typically presented at ranges of about 8 to 12 yards. I see no reason however why the rod should not be capable of the downstream presentation of both wet and dry flies where the rivers are not too large and the rules permit it.

Generally the rod subdued its fish quite satisfactorily though on one occasion a very vigorous wild river-bred rainbow on the Derbyshire Wye got downstream in a fast deep well oxygenated flow and it had to be removed by main force when all attempts at subtlety had failed as a great scrum of bushes prevented my downstream progress. This put a most impressive bend (or alarming to me as the rod's maker) in the rod, a state of affairs which was further not helped by the short handled net I was using that required the fish be brought very close for enmeshing. This was a situation that precluded the imaginative use of the rod that will be referred to in the paragraphs to come and although a rod must be able to withstand this sort of usage occasionally it is best avoided if at all possible on a regular basis. Despite this 'fright' during its first season of use I was pleased with the rod's performance as it demonstrated in the short term that it had been adequately made as any significant faults would most likely have revealed themselves quite quickly. Its long term future however is dependent on a number of factors that are to a large extent controllable, some of which are outlined below and can reasonably be listed under the heading of care of the rod, and others such as the quality of the bamboo which are rather in the lap of the gods; sometimes a rod made from a culm as carefully chosen as any other may in the long run exhibit less staying power than one might expect for no obvious reason.

An important feature and maybe the most important one affecting the life of any rod and in particular one of bamboo is how it is cared for in both the active and passive phases of its life as even an excellently made item can be harmed if not used with imagination; the critical question here however is what does 'with imagination' mean? The best I can do is to suggest a number of guidelines/rules that might fall under the general heading of 'imaginative use', some of which are obvious and others that are less so.

For example, the rod should be used in a manner that spreads the load over as much of its length as possible and thus avoids putting too much of a bend in its finer parts whether during casting, false casting or landing a fish. Severe stress, in a simplistic way, can be defined as bending a rod to such a degree that part of it deforms and is thus taken beyond

The long bow-handled net comfortably in place

its elastic limit to the extent that no amount of remedial work will eliminate the bend that is caused, i.e. it is permanent, or of course breaks the rod. In pursuit of this end, allied with experiences such as that of the downstream rainbow outlined above, the long bow-handled net shown on the previous page was made and the short handled variety set aside when bamboo was used. Short handled scoop type nets are excellent in many respects, particularly in terms of convenience, but I tend to think of them complementing carbon rather than bamboo rods; maybe their development occurred concurrently with such rods. The long handle allows a fish to be netted 'at distance' (see page 82) with the rod held more or less parallel to the water so keeping a large and thus harmless angle between rod and line which greatly reduces the stress on the rod generally and on its finer parts in particular. To be able to enmesh a fish without having to take the rod top behind one's shoulder is very beneficial and a factor that should also be kept in mind, particularly if a fish has to be brought to hand for release when no net is available. It also eliminates the need for extending collapsible or folding nets that can sometimes have a tendency to misfire usually at some crucial moment. However despite the benefits to the rod the long handle is not so convenient as the short, an inconvenience that is partly offset by the bow in the net's handle that allows it to fit more conveniently and comfortably across the back than a straight handled one of the same length. My friends however are inclined to think that it has something to do with all the years of bowmaking that have taken place and they may well be right. As an exercise in lamination making the net was interesting.

Bamboo rods ought to be used in venues where the fish that can reasonably be expected to be caught are in their 'weight category'. Failure to do this habitually will lead to two evils in which both the rod and the fish suffer. The rod will lose its crispness and become flaccid in action and will cease to be pleasant to use long before its time – in short it will have the stuffing knocked out of it – and the fish will be brought to the net in such an exhausted state that its survival after release is jeopardised (lactic acid and all that). If however a really fine specimen is hooked then by careful playing the rod should not come to any harm and if at the end of day after the landing of such a fish the rod exhibits a slight bend then allow it to rest on a flat surface overnight whereupon the curvature is likely to have disappeared. As long as use does not spill over into abuse all will be well. Wand-like carbon rods are sometimes esteemed because of their ability to subdue large fish but this they may do more as a result of their 'indestructible' qualities rather than their ability to sufficiently pressurise a fish so as to allow it to be netted quickly. I am not wholly sure where the kudos lies in totally exhausting a fish even if it is to be retained, but this is a personal feeling though one that may have some merit particularly in this day and age when some field sports are coming under increasing pressure and fishing may well do so at some point in the future. Consideration given to the strength of the tippet used with a bamboo rod is probably more critical than with modern carbon rods which are so strong that the only limiting factor really need be the thickness of material necessary to fool the fish into taking the fly; a lighter tippet tends to disincline one from hauling too hard so a measure of protection is afforded to the rod allied of course with the idea of staying within the rod's 'fish weight category'. I should indicate at this point that I think that carbon rods are wonderful examples of modern technology and that our sport has been greatly enhanced by their development. I use them frequently and get much pleasure from doing so.

Just as fish size should be considered so should line size as a rod that is constantly used with too heavy a line will suffer unless this is done for a specific purpose, e.g. where very short casts are required. This usage will not affect a rod to the same degree as one that is constantly outgunned by big fish but it will tire it in a way that no amount of rest will wholly reinvigorate. Conversely a rod paired with too light a line (unless the casts required are very long) will get thrashed about in a manner that will shake its teeth loose as action is demanded of it. This thrashing often manifests itself by the appearance of stress rings on the ferrule bindings which are areas that are subject to considerable stress. Indeed even when a line of the correct size is being aerialised it is best to gently coax the action out of a rod rather than wildly crack it like a whip until sufficient weight of line is airborne to make it work properly. Indeed one of my pet dislikes is to see a rod vigorously wiggled about with no line to work against which I regard as more or less synonymous with drawing and releasing a bow without an arrow, an action that is likely to cause a wooden bow to simply explode.

In addition to the above points and cases of obvious abuse – craning fish over bankside vegetation or squeezing the assembled rod into a car too short for the purpose, etc., which most will agree are very bad things but are all likely to be guilty of in the heat of the moment – there are some seemingly innocuous things that can seriously damage a rod. Here are two 'for examples'. I was once asked to make a new top for a rod that had been broken when its owner had attempted to free a fly that was anchored in an apparently insignificant bush by flicking at it with the rod. This type of action can put very great stress on a rod for an instant, particularly if the leader and knots are sound even when the tippet is of low breaking strain; the top section in this case had snapped cleanly through. Another angler put a really impressive permanent bend in his rod when pulling the leader through the rings in readiness for attaching the fly. The leader/line knot jammed in a ring and with the hand holding the leader close to the handle he gave it a jerk to free it causing the top of the rod to keel over about 12" from the tip in a very impressive and permanent manner. One may think that rods should be able to withstand such things, and frequently they seem to, but they are best avoided particularly if one tends towards the unlucky; lucky guys seem to be able to do all these things with impunity, but then some people win the Lottery. Fortunately neither of these rods were made by me as both anglers were very aggrieved that they had damaged their rods 'so easily'; clearly their Lottery chances are not good!

Ferrules should be maintained and serviced so that they are easy to operate and do not require great force to engage with one another or take apart. Assuming that they slide smoothly together, as they should, then this situation can be maintained if they are cleaned before and after use and a stopper is employed to keep out dust/grit, etc. when the rod is dormant; a stopper should also be long enough to protect the tip section when the rod is stored in its bag. If a ferrule does jam then try to avoid twisting the rod sections to disengage it; it is a great help if rubber kitchen gloves are worn to afford a firm grip so that the force can be applied linearly rather than with a twisting motion that is likely to wring the rod's neck; once apart the problem should be rectified (see Session 13).

During the passive stages of a rod's life there are some things that can be done to make it comfortable and content. Although storing a rod badly is unlikely to bring about its demise in the dramatic manner outlined above it will cause a steady deterioration. To stay straight and in good condition it should be hung in its bag from a high peg and not left as one unit and rested against a wall or laid horizontally on insufficient supports. Continuous gentle pressure will deform a bamboo rod quite noticeably. Keeping the wet out of and off a rod is important, not in the sense of being paranoid about getting it wet on a fishing trip, which is the job of its finish, but on a long term basis. Over time the protective finish will become compromised through general wear and tear – scuffs of one type or another and fly strike (of one sort anyway) some of which will be deep enough to let the wet reach the rod fibres. Such blemishes are best addressed quickly in the short term by the application of a quick drying waterproof finish (clear nail or fly head varnishes for example) until a long term solution can be adopted; really deep nicks however might need more than just a new coating of varnish. Thoroughly drying the rod and its bag separately prior to storing it away in a warm, dry place at say living room temperature will be appreciated by the rod rather as it is by humans; long term wet or damp will progressively lift the edges of a wound, stain the surface and eventually rot the fibres. If this procedure cannot be carried out when say camping out then wiping it down thoroughly is an alternative that will pay dividends over time. Warm is OK but objects made from natural materials are best not stored in extremely hot places as prolonged exposure to high temperatures can prove very enervating and sort of dry out even apparently dry objects, so avoid boiler rooms, roof spaces, etc. and vehicles in summertime especially if you live in a hot place. Quite what harm will occur in such places is difficult to predict precisely: modern glues should be unaffected but on one rod that had lived in the roof space for quite some time one summer the ferrules loosened and had to be refixed so something had shrunk; not a disaster but best avoided. Certainly an extremely dried out wooden bow should be treated with great caution if you value your head.

All this advice and 'Dos and Don'ts' may incline you to think that bamboo rods are hugely sensitive creatures that are ready to collapse at the slightest whiff of misuse which however is not always the case. I have seen and sometimes been asked to rejuvenate rods that have had none of the foregoing advice applied to them so they looked in the most parlous state and seemed to require the attention of a magician rather than a rod restorer. Some of these rods however were encouraged in various ways to live and fight another day. The most recent of these, which had apparently spent decades in a damp garden shed and was restored on the understanding (or so I thought) that it would be used only for small fry, accounted for a 5lb sea trout on the river Dart near Ashburton in Devon one dark summer's night; a true Lazarus of a rod.

Quite how long a bamboo rod will go on performing with its full vigour even when used 'properly' must depend on various factors such as the quality of the raw material which, being natural, is bound to vary, the time that it is in active use as opposed to lying dormant in the rod cabinet and what that 'active use' comprises. For example, a rod that is used by a very active angler who habitually searches the water for a largely unseen quarry will see more active service of the casting sort in a given time than one used by a stalker who casts only occasionally to observed feeding fish. Similarly a highly successful angler who catches many more and larger fish than another will subject his rod to much more hard work of the fish landing sort within a given period. It was established in the early years of last century by a famous American bowyer and bow hunter, Dr Saxton Pope, that a traditionally designed yew long bow made from a top class stave was 'in its prime' for about 100,000 shots after which its powers would diminish noticeably, the diminution being clearly apparent because the bow could not shoot an arrow so far as formerly. I am not sure that bamboo rods can be tested in such a precise way as bows which are drawn (pulled back) a given amount for each shot into a more highly stressed state than is likely with a sensibly used bamboo rod ('a bow full drawn is $7/8$ broken') or have their lessening powers so easily observed. The demands on rods are more variable, variables touched on above – the casting action of the angler, the length of line cast, the type and size of fish subdued, etc. The 20 outings made by the Diary Rod in its first season were made up of 15 full days and 5 half days during which it was probably in active use for at least 100 hours as a result of my seeming inability to sit and wait quietly for a hatch of fly that may or may not happen which in turn may or may not generate a rise of fish; having usually travelled many miles to a river, simply sitting by it is not enough and anyway I enjoy the action of casting. From this you will be correct in deducing that the rod was used to search the water for some period of time on each of its outings and although it was my intention of keeping an accurate count of the number of casts made on a typical day at some point in the process I always lost the plot. During the season however I cannot conceive that the rod made less than many thousands (5, 6, 7?)

of fly delivering casts and accompanying false casts which resulted in the fish mentioned above being hooked, none of which (not even the rainbow) took it near the '⅞ broken' stage, so everything that happened to it can be classed as use and not abuse. At the end of the season there appeared to be no diminution in its capacities and though one season should not be sufficient time to cause this to happen it probably is long enough to expose weaknesses of one sort or another. I suspect however that any item used in a dynamic way, particularly those made of natural materials, will 'let down' over time. Wooden bows almost always develop some degree of set when unstrung and lose a few pounds of pull after they have shot a few dozen arrows. They are said to 'follow the string' and provided that this is not too pronounced one just ignores it (which is only sensible as there is nothing effective that can be done about it). Some bamboo rods will do the same and, just as with bows, it is best to forget about it as there is rarely any wholly effective way of eliminating the slight curve; some try putting the rings on the convex side of the bend or try heat treatment which will work for a while but the weakness that caused the rod to take slight curve in one direction will soon manifest itself again and bend it the opposite way. Provided the curve is even and spread over a substantial length of rod it will do no great harm and is probably just a feature of the particular bamboo that was used to make the rod and not a fault in the making per se. It is still likely to catch plenty of fish. Sharp, nasty permanent angles however are something different and might well indicate poor workmanship or taper or both. I have some rods that were made many years ago (more than 30 in some cases) that still seem to perform and look as well as ever but maybe this is just a trick of the light and really we have simply grown older together and neither of us wants to admit to this inevitable fact; don't older blokes think that inside there is still a 20 year old trying to get out despite what the mirror tells them daily? With luck and a following wind this season I shall occasionally set aside my carbon reservoir rods to take a particular 9'4" #7 line Stillwater/sea trout rod to Blagdon Lake in the Mendips where it accounted for a limit of beautiful rainbows one evening in the broiling summer of 1976 where we shall try to repeat the performance; I will have to be lucky to do so well but if I don't it won't be the rod's fault I am sure. What is certain is that with its full or even diminishing power a well made and imaginatively used bamboo rod will catch fish for decades and maybe more than one lifetime.

1a Water Lane
Flitwick
Beds

2nd December 1976

Dear Mr Strang,

I was most interested to read your letter in the current issue of Angling. It's fun to make your own split cane rods, and I hope you won't think that with glass and carbon fibre now available, there is no longer a place for the split cane rod. I for one still use cane, specially for accurate casting on rivers of modest size.

If you intend making quite a number of rods, it might be worth considering making, or having made, a milling machine. All you need is an electric motor of about ¼ horsepower with a spindle machined so that it can take a milling cutter, and some device for grinding a wooden or metal former, with a 60 degree apex as per Lawton Moss, past the cutter in a straight line. There are many simple ways of doing this, and the result is a saving of time, and greatly improved accuracy.

Good luck to your endeavours!

Richard Walker

Richard Walker

When I received this letter from Richard Walker in the early years of my rod making I was very pleased and impressed that someone so esteemed in the angling world as a catcher of record fish, prolific writer, rod designer and general innovator should take the trouble to put pen to paper and communicate with me, a total unknown. Clarissa his (then) record carp of 44lbs lived for many years in the aquarium at London Zoo where I saw her swimming contentedly about in retirement having been caught on his famous Mark IV split bamboo carp rod, facsimiles of which I was subsequently able to make (see page 48). Such rods can of course be used for other sorts of fish that grow to a great size - pike, salmon, barbel, etc. - for which they still command the interest of a small number of fishermen who enjoy using rods of a natural material just as do some trout fishers.

In addition to the general pleasure the receipt of the letter gave me, I still remember clearly the sense of encouragement it engendered at a time when contact with other rod makers was greatly more restricted than it is today. When Richard Walker passed away at a relatively early age angling in the UK lost one of its most significant participants, maybe the most significant of the 20th century.

Spliced rod joints – bamboo to go!

A fly fishing friend of mine manages the game department of the premier tackle shop in the city where I am sure he is good at all aspects of his job and rather too good at some. One of these strengths is getting me to part with my money for items he convinces me I cannot do without. Some of these essential items have included some expensive 4-piece carbon Traveller rods and as I am not a wanderer on the world stage you will appreciate his prowess as a salesman or my gullibility – no surely not the latter, or so I try to vainly reassure myself. Anyway his salesmanship or my inability to resist a shiny new toy means I now have quite a collection of these multipiece rods so wherever it is that I am supposed to be going the fish had better watch out as I'll be ready for them!

Be all that as it may as a maker of bamboo rods it always seems the 'right thing' to do to catch a few fish with the split bamboo whenever and wherever I find myself, particularly if a river is being visited for the first time. Thus the idea of transporting cane rods as conveniently as carbon made me wonder if multipiece bamboo rods were a possibility. This set me on a journey, not of the travelling sort but in my head, to try and foresee any obvious (and maybe insurmountable) problems before anything practicable was attempted. From this head scratching the first thing to emerge was that to try and make a rod in the conventional form would be hopeless as such a rod would contain about as much metal as the tank aerials that were so prized when I was a boy in the years just after WW2 and little else in the rod line was available. Maybe hopeless is too stark and dismissive a word but the thought of fitting all those ferrules was enough to put me off. Consequently the notion of 'wood to wood' joints (grass to grass really) presented itself, spliced joints secured with some sort of tape that were sometimes found on bamboo and greenheart rods in years gone by but are rarely (never?) seen today.

As I had not made a spliced rod of any sort in my then thirty years of rod making (the initial Traveller having been made about a decade ago) the thought of plunging in and attempting to make a four piecer straight off seemed a little rash so I dipped my toe so to speak by making an 8'0" two-part hexagonally sectioned rod with a taper that had produced a number of excellent rods in the past with obviously just the one joint. The rod was made in my usual way, apart of course from the ferrule fitting using wooden preparation boards

Netting 'at distance' with a 3-piece spliced joint rod

and the adjustable steel variety to produce the splines so that after a few weeks the rod was ready for its trial run. However in my eagerness to try it out (childishness really) I could not be bothered to get any proper splicing tape so I used ordinary masking tape instead and discovered that it worked beautifully. I still haven't got any 'proper stuff' but keep promising that I will... soon (!) if indeed it is still available, though I guess that anything that does the job properly can be deemed 'proper stuff '.

Having been designed for small to medium size rivers I took the rod to a place I know well where there was every chance of a fish or two as a bit of early success always gives one some confidence in new gear. As it happens things turned out even better than I could reasonably have hoped as on its very first cast in earnest (and here you will just have to take my word for it) a respectable trout of 14″ took a PT nymph, fought well, was netted, photographed and released which made me think that there really must be something in this spliced rod lark and do you know that that thought turned out to be quite correct! More trial outings followed which established the idea/design as perfectly satisfactory after which there was no excuse for not pressing ahead with the multipiece version.

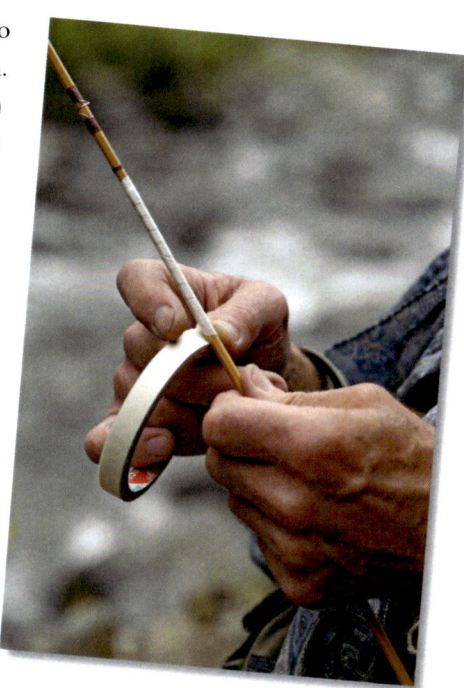

A few things had to be sorted out but it was essentially a case of applying what had been learned from making the 2-piece rod and taking my cue from the 4-sectioned carbon rods already mentioned, I stuck with the idea of making of a 4-piece bamboo rod rather than complicating the issue further by increasing the number of sections, though one could if there was some pressing reason for doing so. Set out below are some of the details that were adopted for the initial construction and some of the subsequent developments.

The taper of the 'datum line' two-piece rod was one that if joined in the standard fashion with a ferrule would ideally require a Swiss type ferrule, i.e. it was a taper that had no marked step down in diameter where the butt and tip portions of the rod entered their respective parts of the ferrule as is sometimes encountered in some rod designs. Although rods exhibiting this feature can work well I avoided it as it may have presented a problem when trying to tape together a joint with a very steeply reducing/increasing diameter over the 4″ of the splice; subsequent experimentation however showed that this was an unwarranted concern.

Each of the four sections had to be made longer than one quarter of the total 8′0″ length of the rod to accommodate the overlap at the splices which were to be made 4″ long tapering to just less than $\frac{1}{32}$″. To allow for the 2″ overlap either side of the mid point of each splice the top and butt sections would both be 26″ long and the two central sections 28″ each. It might be impressive to write that the length of the splices was established in a highly technical manner but this was not the case: it was just that 5″ looked too long and 3″ too short so I split the difference and made them 4″, which as luck would have it was a good choice. The end of the splice is as has been indicated, about $\frac{1}{32}$″ thick which seems about right, any thicker and it will not 'marry' well with the rest of the splice and look clumsy and any thinner makes it rather too fragile for practical use.

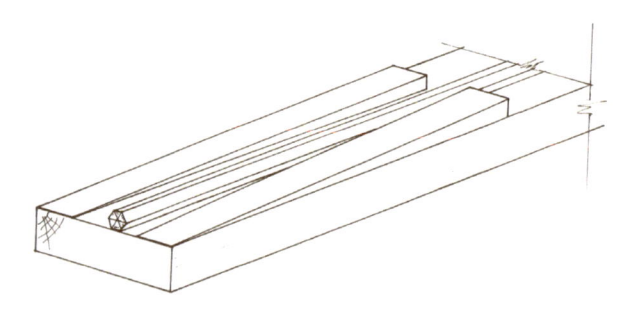

The splices were cut from the 'normal' diameters of the rod and were not swelled for reinforcement purposes at these points as was frequently seen on rods from bygone ages since I wanted the rod to bend in as even a manner as possible which would be unlikely if there were three stiff portions along its length... more of this later. Initially the splices were tapered with the aid of a wedge-shaped jig that allowed the rod section to lie between its sloping elements and to be clamped gently but firmly in position well clear of the planing action. When subsequent trials showed that the splices could be successfully done 'by eye' the jig was set aside. This was achieved by clamping the section (gently!) on a board of say 1"x 3" x 30" with a line marked across the width which indicates where the splice has to commence. Planing by eye made the creation of a splice a little easier than with the jig as each splice requires a slightly different angle due to the different diameters at each joint if a splice length of 4" was to be achieved, e.g. a more acute angle at the tip than say at the butt which in theory at least means that a wedge of a different angle is required for each joint. Whichever method is employed the end of the rod section must be aligned flush with the end of the jig/board so that the forward stroke of the plane can be made in an unimpeded manner along the full length of the splice and 'off' the end of the base board. If things are not arranged in this manner the front of the plane will hit the base board before a full length shaving of the splice can be made. If you wish a quick way of removing the majority of the waste can be devised – fine band saw, dovetail saw or even a knife if you feel brave enough. I do not find planing the splines by eye too difficult as I have made literally dozens of hand planed arrows from square sectioned (½"x ½") battens as I have been a bow (and arrow) maker for longer than I have been a rod maker. I do not think however that someone who has made a few rods should have any problem with this method though I accept that there will be those who are more content to use a jig. The jig works on the same principle as the one used for splicing bamboo strips in preparation for making splines but of course these splices are cut on the rod's longitudinal axis whereas the others are cut laterally.

The rod section lies between the two sloping elements of the jig. The bamboo must be clamped well clear of the plane

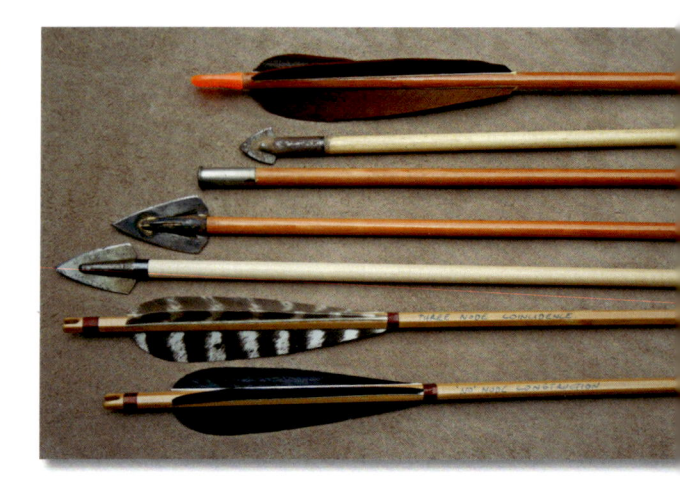

A selection of hand planed arrows in a variety of woods with the two being made from split bamboo which looked very fine but were rather heavy

Some splices showing that no reinforcement is applied at the joint which can be firmly secured with masking tape

Any fine adjustments that may be required to the splice face after planing can be done on a squared block (say 10"x 3"x 2") with abrasive paper glued to one face – 80 grit is OK – that can be held level in the bench vice so the splice face can be rubbed on it in a controlled manner. Once the splices have been checked for quality and all is correct (which can be established by taping the joints together) the ends should be rounded somewhat as 'corners' are prone to catch in things – coat cuffs, rod bags, etc. – and the sharp side edges dulled off for much the same reasons.

When cutting the first splice, which for no very good reason I always seem to do on the top section, its orientation in respect of the face of the hexagon to which the guides/rings are fixed I have found to be of no consequence, i.e. the 'slope' can be towards or away from the 'ring' face. Thereafter the splices are cut parallel to this initial orientation as shown in the diagram below.

It seems not to matter whether the guides/rings are put on face A or B in relation to the way in which the splices are cut

The adjustable steel or wooden boards are set in the usual manner with care being taken to mark the places where the splices occur as here the splines must have the same taper – nothing difficult but probably worth mentioning. I will not regale readers again with a blow by blow account of making the rod; suffice to say that it included a number of idiosyncrasies that have crept into my rod making mostly from bowmaking by a sort of osmosis which have helped to simplify certain parts of the process in particular and the whole affair in general, but then I am sure that I am not alone in having personal foibles in this respect. And here an interesting anomaly presents itself, at least it does if you are both a bamboo rod and bow maker in the amateur setting as it is possible for the hobbyist with (usually) limited resources to make a modern take-apart bow even to the point of casting an aluminium handle, an item that equates to a modern carbon Traveller rod which in the normal scheme of things is not within the scope of the amateur rod maker. However making a multipiece wooden bow, which is the equivalent of a bamboo Traveller rod, is not usually a feasible proposition (not wholly impossible but not really worth the effort). Anyway back to rods, the addition of rings, handle, reel seat, etc., all of which took about 24–25 hours of working time, left me with the first multipiece rod of its sort that I had ever seen.

How did the rod perform? Well, very well is the honest answer even allowing for any parental bias I might have entertained. It had/has a positive and pleasant action that was not noticeably different from the rod on which it had been modelled, its action being a function of its taper not its multipiecedness which has allowed it to be used continuously throughout numerous days' fishing and end up as willing as at the start. It has not accounted for any very large fish, the best being a 2lb/17″ wild brown trout, a good fish for the river where it was caught and released to fight another day but clearly no monster. This fish was the largest I have ever caught on that particular water thus the rod obviously did not hamper my efforts in taking a fish as big as I seem capable of fooling. The longest day of sustained and continuous work it has had to endure lasted the whole of an autumn day during which the grayling I was after exhibited a near suicidal quality that seemed to lead them to believe that anything, even metal adorned with fur and feather, that passed close to them was food; dozens were caught and released. At the close of play all that had happened was that the masking tape had become a bit soggy but by then so had I as the result of the occasional dunking and the odd shower of rain which did not reflect badly on the rod per se or me for that matter.

I did discover after a few outings that it was necessary to protect the splices where they are bound with tape with a two-part cellulose (resin and hardener) system of the sort that can be bought from model aircraft shops or wood merchants.

This finish resists much better the peeling action on the rod finish that occurs when the tape is removed than the polyurethane with which I initially protected them. Indeed one reason for continuing to use masking tape rather than say sellotape, which is much stronger, is that this type of tape sticks so fiercely that it is capable of removing pretty well any finish apart maybe from an impregnated one and even then it may attempt to consume the rod splinter by splinter. You could of course combine the two and put a layer of this tape over the masking tape if you felt the joint needed extra support. I have never used electrical insulating tape which is sometimes suggested as it creates a thick and unsightly joint. Also a very tough finish on the splices probably helps to physically protect these quite delicate parts in a general sense – just marginally I guess.

I also wondered after a while if some 'unseen' things might be happening in the joints that would not occur in metal ferruled rods. Close inspection did reveal very slight friction marks on the contact faces of the splices which indicated that there must be some longitudinal 'give' during use; of lateral movement I could find no evidence. However none of this 'movement' was discernable during any of the rod's functions – false casting, casting, playing a fish, etc. – and I suspect that any joint of this sort secured in this way will be subject to some degree of 'give'. This scrutiny I found encouraging as it indicated that 4" splices were wholly adequate for the purpose when secured with a single spiral of tightly applied ½" wide tape in which each turn overlaps its predecessor by half the tape's width and with the ends of the splices being given a couple of extra turns to prevent 'lifting'.

The benefits of these rods fall into a number of categories. For example, they offer all the convenience of their modern counterparts – ease of transport, use as a back-up rod and maybe not least because they can be locked in the boot/trunk of the car away from prying eyes which is probably a sad indictment of some aspects of today's society. For the rod maker they offer the possibility of creating a 'new' rod with a different action by changing the taper of say the tip section or the butt or both for use with the original middle parts, which requires less effort than making a whole new rod. When changing a rod's specification in this manner – let's say increasing or decreasing the butt dimensions to alter the rod's line rating – it is probably best to restrict the alteration to just one line size, e.g. 5 to 6, 5 to 4, etc. Making bigger jumps may introduce problems. In terms of durability well constructed spliced rods are as good as the conventional type: when tensioned the whole rod assumes a lovely curve right through the splices which become an integral part of the bend so that the stress is spread throughout the 'active' part of the rod, a length which will vary depending on which type of taper you selected. The first rod was of semi parabolic nature so that most of the material outside the handgrip was sharing the load. This 'whole bend' can be readily observed if the arched rod is sighted against a straight edge such as that formed between the junction of a wall and a ceiling: this feature pleased me as it gave purpose to the idea of not swelling/reinforcing the joints and thus creating flat spots as indeed would a whole host of ferrules. Making as much of a rod as possible active is an idea that came from bow making as the durability of traditional wooden long bows was greatly enhanced by having dips cut either side of the handgrip, i.e. material was removed from these points thus allowing more of the limbs to bend when the bow was drawn and so share the strain. This was of great benefit as the old adage 'a bow full drawn is $7/8$ broken' is true, indeed some would say that $9/10$ is nearer the mark. Although most rods are rarely so highly stressed I still tend to favour rods of semi or parabolic action and to avoid those that swell markedly just above the handgrip despite knowing about the concept of keeping the thrust ahead of the hand. Also I dislike the idea of having say an 8'0" rod tip actioned of which only about 7' is active and of this length the finest parts might be subjected to considerable stress due to the 'stiff as a poker' butt that just acts as a lever. However, be that as it may, an advantage that did not occur to me when I set out on the Traveller journey was that dealing with the much shorter rod sections – binding, straightening, removing twists, etc. – was much easier than with their longer 'normal' counterparts. And finally regarding the benefits, it offers those who have made a number of conventional rods the opportunity of venturing on a new project that will produce an eminently practicable fishable rod that might also become a talking point.

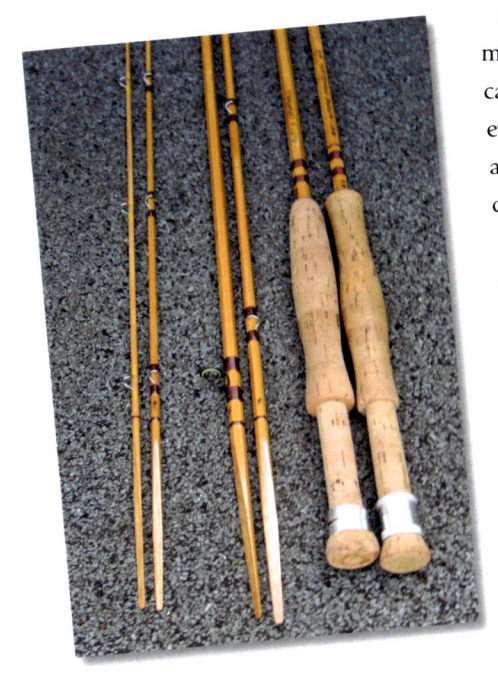

However where there are pluses there are likely to be some minuses and of course this is the case here also. For example, care has to be taken not to damage the fine ends of the splices even during storage so protective tips are necessary, the most appropriate and smartest being made from short ends of built cane. The rods take longer and a bit more care to assemble and take down than their conventional peers and of course you ABSOLUTELY MUST NOT leave the splicing tape back at base – I haven't done so yet but just give me time...! Making rods with more than four sections might prove tricky and thus be deemed a minus due to at least one very fine splice being required though a 4-piece 6'0" rod for a #4 line which required splices to be cut in fine diameters has been made; a 5-piece 8'0" rod would be unlikely to require finer work. I bet however that there would be a frantic scramble if you arrived at a water just as the hatch was ending and you had to assemble your 5-piece rod: who would succeed without resorting to profanity?

Two 4-piece rods based on the same two mid sections which are matched with the (two) different tips and butts to create one rod for use with a #5 line and another for a #6

Once a few Travellers had been made and proved really good tools the thought of actually making rods in two or three pieces without having to fit ferrules (a job I really dislike) became more and more attractive and so the collection of spliced jointers, like Topsey, mustard seeds, acorns, etc., grew and grew so that there are now rods ranging from 6'0" to 9'0" for a variety of line sizes. A 3-piece 8'0" for a #5 line has proved very popular with my friends falling as it does between the (relative) inconvenience of transporting a 2-piecer and the extra time required in assembling the Traveller. We have used these rods for a decade or so now so I am perfectly at ease with this type of joint which seems to me to be infinitely preferable to cluttering up a rod with a whole pile of metal.

The 'whole rod bend' is apparent here

Here are the sizes for an 8'0" #5 rod that as a project can be made in two, three and four pieces with spliced joints and in one piece though why anyone, me included, would want such an inconvenient rod goodness knows... As you might guess I have 'the complete set'! Where there are two values on the butt section diameters (from the 75" mark) the smaller ones are for the #5 line and the larger for a #6.

0"	5"	10"	15"	20"	25"	30"	35"	40"
0.078"	0.093"	0.108"	0.125"	0.142"	0.155"	0.169"	0.187"	0.203"

45"	50"	55"	60"	65"	70"
0.224"	0.242"	0.258"	0.270"	0.283"	0.287"

75"	80"	85"	90"	96"
0.290" (0.294")	0.294" (0.300")	0.305" (0.310")	310" (0.314")	0.315" (0.318)

Section lengths   4-piece, 2 @ 26", 2 @ 28"
                  3-piece, 2 @ 34", 1 @ 36"
                  2-piece, 2 @ 50"

Handle and reel seat – 10"

Weight – about 4ozs or a shade less

Action tending towards parabolic

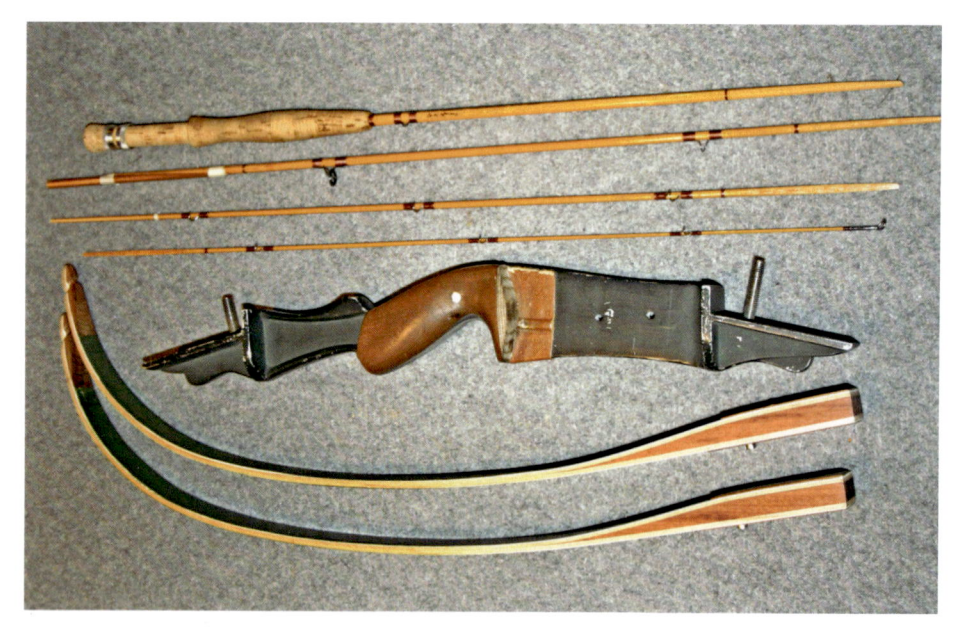

Take-apart bows that were first made in the workshop 25 years ago also probably influenced the decision to make multipiece rods. And just as such rods can be altered to produce different actions so can the weight (pull) of the bows by substituting different limbs

88 | **Spliced rod joints – bamboo to go!** | The diary of a rod

Some approaches to designing a rod

Just as initially the notion of making a split bamboo rod from basic materials seemed a rather daunting task so at first did the idea of designing one when the desire to expand the involvement in the craft beyond the stage of just physically making rods was reached. This apprehension was caused in part by the regiments of figures and calculations that marched across numerous pages of some publications under the design process banner and particularly so for someone without an extensive background in mathematics and engineering.

However, as things transpired, these initial deficits on my part did not prove insurmountable obstacles to gradually becoming increasingly familiar with the rod tapers which in my mind are pretty well synonymous with rod design with all other things being deemed less important. Whether one should think in this way is open to question (one probably shouldn't) but it has sufficed for me for a long time now so I am disinclined to change on this point. That which follows below is pretty much a chronological account of how I came to have some sort of tenuous of grip on this slippery subject.

The first option is simply to (apparently) ignore the whole design process per se and be content with making copies of existing rods, the data for which can be obtained by measuring any rod that comes to hand with a micrometer and tape measure and/or by getting it from publications and now the Internet. It is probably hard to avoid this approach at first as, with no designing experience, where else does one start, assuming one is working alone which is frequently the case when one is not well versed enough in the mathematical and engineering knowledge to allow one to proceed straightaway with design? However although this approach avoids or appears to avoid the design process in a conscious manner it is likely that a basic appreciation of some of its aspects will be absorbed by a sort of osmosis whereby information and understanding leak into one's understanding, particularly if one is imaginative about what is going on and does not simply block out such considerations. For example, it will be quickly realised that a rod section has only to be made marginally thicker for it to become very much stiffer without the rod maker having any knowledge of the mathematics that illustrate this point; a piece of bamboo that is twice as thick as another will be about eight times as stiff. I was not wholly unaware of this feature when the first few rods were being made because of my bow making as bow limbs are subject to exactly the same laws (as is every other sort of beam). However despite an appreciation of this factor one can be caught out – I have one pair of bow limbs that I am barely able to draw (pull back) due to insufficient attention being paid to this important point; in this instance the cores of the limbs were made just a few thou too thick. So over time the measurements (lengths/diameters) and the physical weight of rods will begin to give one an idea of their likely line rating and the sort of action they will have.

The second 'design' possibility is to add or change some feature of an existing rod to suit your own taste – not fundamental aspects like diameters or lengths but such things as handgrips, reel seatings or maybe the substitution of a higher class of ferrule, a different type of finish. Some of these are cosmetic things but as attractive appearance or less weight are elements of design then a claim can be made that some involvement in the design process has taken place albeit at the margins. One fly fisher I heard about and met briefly had, I think, a desire to become a rod maker but his (it was a he) ambitions were never wholly realised; the nearest he got to split bamboo rod making it seems was to buy really expensive rods, strip off the rings and the varnish and replace them with his own handiwork which obviously gave him a sense of achievement and closer involvement with his equipment. Apparently a number of his rods received this treatment, despite costing many hundreds of pounds each and all went well until one that he had completed was being given a trial on the lawn when he was called in to lunch. When lunch was over he went out and started to mow the lawn, quite forgetting that the rod with some line extended was lying on the grass.

He 'came to' as the mower was in the act of consuming first the line and then the rod as he despairingly tried to turn it off. A friend who witnessed the result of this gruesome business reported that all that was left when the machine was brought to a belated halt was the reel seat. The commiserations that were required were very difficult to deliver with a straight face despite the very obvious mortification of the owner who was wondering what could be done about it. There must be a moral in this somewhere but I am sure that you can think of it as easily as I – one conclusion must be that it was a really good lunch!

Over time, after numerous rods with differing actions have been studied and made, it is likely that an empirical sense of design will begin to establish itself as was hinted at earlier if one is receptive to the idea. This will allow more fundamental changes to be made to existing rods – changes in rod action/length, etc. rather than appearance – and lead maybe to the production of wholly 'new' and individual items. No calculations in a mathematical sense will be involved but an intuitive understanding of what alterations in diameter and/or length will be necessary to produce a rod with a particular action aided no doubt by a little trial and error. For example, at a quite simplistic level, using an 8'0" #5 rod as a reference, it will be soon realised that if the diameter of the bamboo is say 0.325–0.330" where it disappears under the cork the rod will feel pretty stiff under the handle; if however the diameter is say 0.310 –0.315" at this point then the action is likely to be semi parabolic and if it is less than that then an even more pronounced butt or through action will be in evidence, figures of course that presuppose that the rest of the rod is correctly proportioned (if they were not then the rod would very likely be for a different line rating).

If long rows of figures seem daunting then expressing them in graph form can literally make the tapers they conceal more visible, making it easier to identify similarities or differences in the tapers of the rods you have plotted. Plotting these graphs made me realise that much of the taper of many rods was based on a straight or nearly straight line, i.e. the diameters at set intervals of (usually but not necessarily) 5" increased so as to produce a straight line. The Diary Rod demonstrates this feature with its taper between 15" and 65" being nearly straight with small deviations occurring either side of this line.

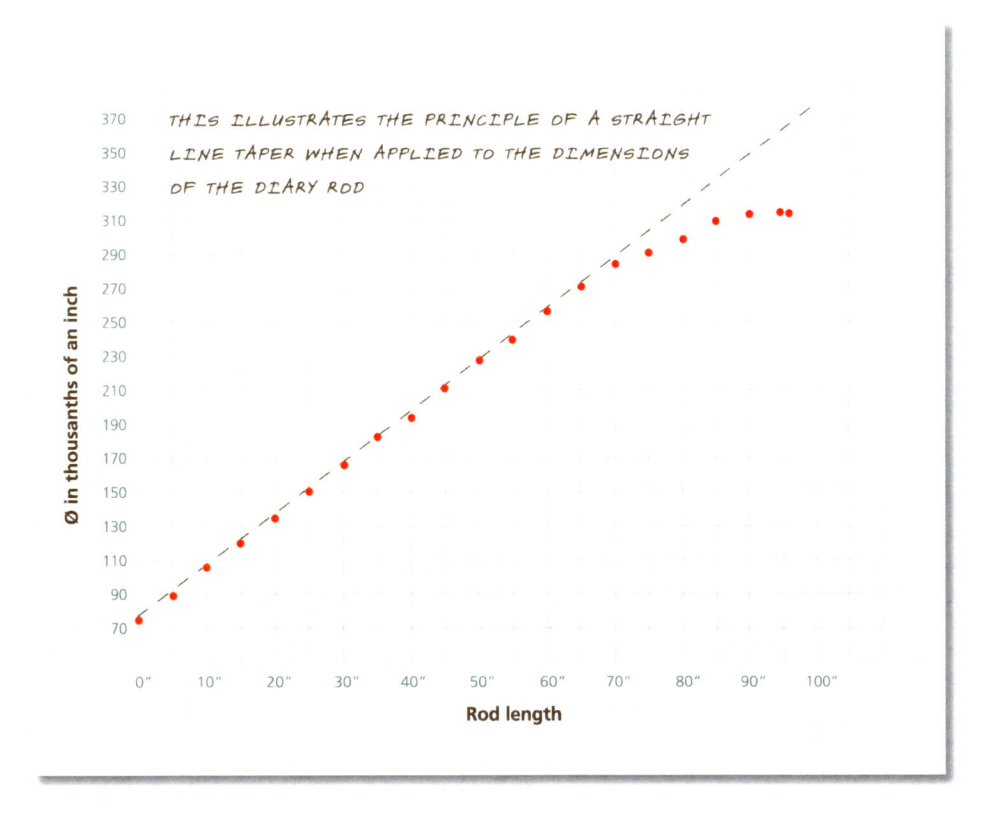

THIS ILLUSTRATES THE PRINCIPLE OF A STRAIGHT LINE TAPER WHEN APPLIED TO THE DIMENSIONS OF THE DIARY ROD

Using this information you can set up a graph with an 'arbitrary' straight line plotted and use this as the basis for creating a rod of your own. Arbitrary is not really the appropriate word as you will by now have a fairly good idea of the starting (tip) and ending values (butt) of the sort of rod you wish to make. For example, if you want to create rods in the 7'6"/8'0" range for lines #5/6 then a line with a starting value at 0" (the tip) of 0.080" and 0.335" at 96" (end of butt) you will have a taper that increases at 0.013" per 5" and thus a datum line from which to work. The straight line taper for the Diary Rod at 15 thou per 5" runs at a little more than this. However by initially keeping say the 'middle' 60–65% of the rod along the straight line and experimenting with the tip and butt portions either side of it you have a fair chance of creating a rod that comes somewhere near that which you want. You must of course remember that lines plotted above and below your straight line will make those parts of the rod stiffer and weaker respectively than one made along the straight line taper. Thus, for example, to create an 8'0" butt or through actioned rod the graph will fall away in a slight curve from about the 70" mark to register a value of about 0.305" where the bamboo disappears under the 10" cork handle; at the other end it is likely to dip marginally from the 15" point to register a tip value of say 0.075". This is a very simplistic method of creating your 'own' rod but it is one that will produce a usable and maybe a very fine rod. Eight examples of the Diary Rod have been made to date using this method of arriving at sensible diameters which have accounted for literally hundreds of fish and are pleasant to cast. Over time in an empirical manner you will arrive at datum straight line tapers that suit your style for rods of varying lengths. Thus if you favour fast actioned rods then you may want to create a straight line that tapers more steeply than 0.013" per 5" which will make the butt stiffer relative to the tip.

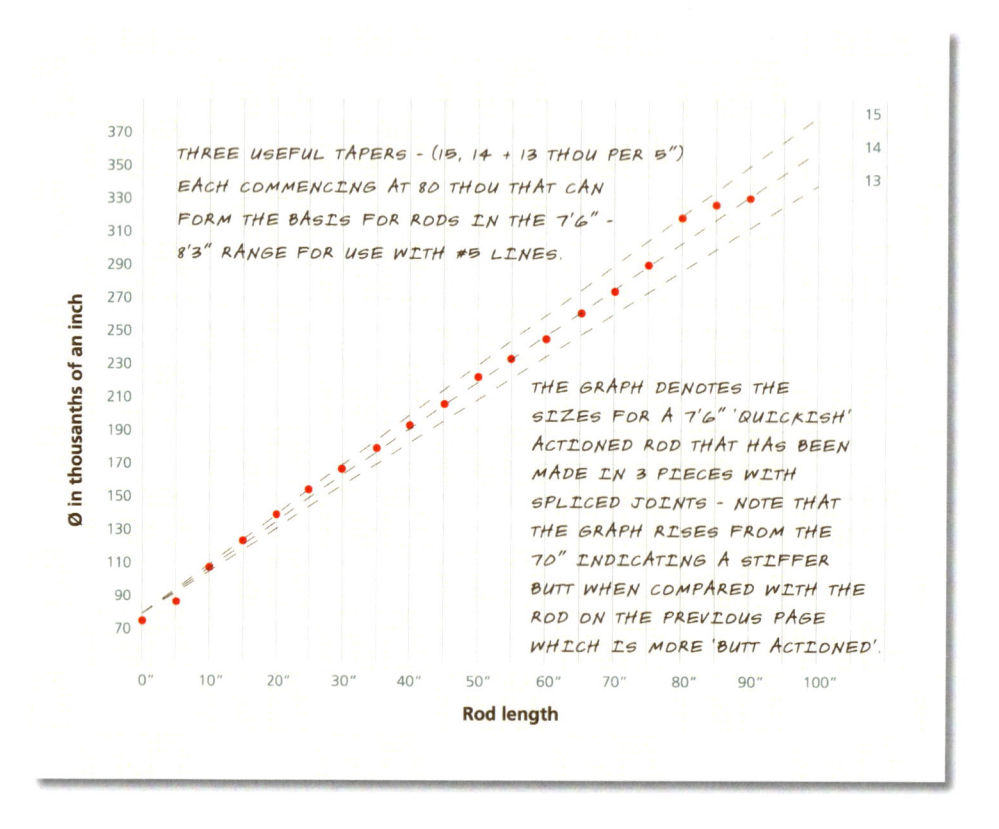

THREE USEFUL TAPERS - (15, 14 + 13 THOU PER 5") EACH COMMENCING AT 80 THOU THAT CAN FORM THE BASIS FOR RODS IN THE 7'6" - 8'3" RANGE FOR USE WITH #5 LINES.

THE GRAPH DENOTES THE SIZES FOR A 7'6" 'QUICKISH' ACTIONED ROD THAT HAS BEEN MADE IN 3 PIECES WITH SPLICED JOINTS - NOTE THAT THE GRAPH RISES FROM THE 70" INDICATING A STIFFER BUTT WHEN COMPARED WITH THE ROD ON THE PREVIOUS PAGE WHICH IS MORE 'BUTT ACTIONED'.

As one collects the data and develops ideas based on the straight line taper suggested above some (possibly) surprising things sometimes come to light. For example, in two-part rods of the same length one tip section when matched with two different butts, one 'thicker' than the other, may well produce rods for use with two different line weights; or two rods say 8'0" and 7'6" respectively may have diameters that are the same down to a point some inches above the handgrip when those of the longer rod will be found to be rather greater but both rods will be for use with the same size line. I have some 3-piece 8'0" rods that make use of this rather neat way of altering a rod's line rating which required only a different butt to be made rather than a whole rod. In theory – or should I say in respect of mathematical exactitude – this should not be the case but in practice such rods can be very fine. Line size it will soon be realised can simply be a guide when a rod is being made as, for example, one fly fisher may use the rod successfully with, let us say, a #5 line whereas another will be content to cast a #6 with it because the former is a more vigorous caster or is someone who habitually aerialises more line than the latter, personal knowledge which the rod builder/designer can make use of when producing a rod for a particular angler. One will also discover that in practice the very minute differences in diameter that are sometimes quoted in publications, whilst probably theoretically correct, have little relevance in practice and are likely to be made redundant by the variation in the quality of bamboo within a culm and from culm to culm as well as making one feel a bit inadequate as a rod builder in a practical sense if one takes them too literally. Certainly one should not be too concerned if a rod works very well but does not match some theoretical or aesthetic norm. These are but some of the examples that make an empirical approach a perfectly acceptable way of proceeding based as it is on hard earned experience and is, I suspect, the way in which many rod makers have created rods that have proved eminently satisfactory.

The next line of approach involves a limited use of mathematical formulae to alter the dimensions of an existing rod to produce one that is say more powerful or longer or different in some other way from the original and is interesting in that it removes what might be called the guesswork inherent in the empirical approach. The formula set out below which relates to the bending of a beam (which in engineering terms is what a rod is) I have found very useful in quite a narrow aspect of rod design and came from the late Richard Walker's book *Rod Building for Amateurs* which, along with the personal interest and encouragement he offered in my initial efforts to make split bamboo fly rods, enabled me to make my first tentative forays into what I regarded as the potentially complex field of rod design. The data relating to the Diary Rod which was designed to cast a #5 line was subjected to this formula so that the diameters for a #6 rod could be calculated with a great degree of certainty. The manner in which this can be done is set out a few pages hence.

$$\frac{wl^3}{d^4}$$

w = weight (line), l = length (of rod),
d = diameter (across flats).

I suppose that the ultimate way of proceeding is to deduce the required sizes with no reference to previously made rods by working from first principles. This requires access to certain information, not least the engineering and mathematical knowledge in addition to the data relating to the material in question, in this case bamboo. If one is not an engineer or mathematician then one is obliged to seek the information from somewhere which in my case was from Garrison and Carmichael's book. It took me some time to pluck up the courage to face the figures but by approaching them a little at a time I found the whole business interesting and ultimately became quite familiar with them. Certainly initially I found myself contemplating things that were unfamiliar, for example – in no particular order – dynamic deformation, forces of bending, allowable stress, weight of the material, centre of gravity, the mathematical formulae, etc. etc. The purpose of the calculations is to ascertain the effect of all the factors that affect the bamboo and are required of it to enable a rod to be made (including the bamboo itself which uses energy to move itself) to arrive at the diameters at equal intervals along a rod's length that will be sufficient to transmit the force generated by the casting action through the rod to cast a length of line of the desired size. Is there any absolute need to gain an understanding of this process? Probably not, however if one makes the effort then a certain confidence is engendered in respect of one's knowledge of rod design even if one does not make habitual use of this knowledge in practice which is the position I find myself in. So unless one is firmly set on mastering the mathematics I am really not very sure that there is any compelling need to wrestle with convoluted calculations: there really is no need to keep on reinventing the wheel.

Rod design is a concept that can be endlessly discussed particularly if those involved are expert in the field of engineering design who can introduce to the subject concepts that in the great scheme of things are not really applicable to the making of a fishing rod though they are in more high-tech spheres. For example, vortex shedding that all objects that move through air or some other medium are subject to isn't at all worth considering in respect of a rod as its effects will be infinitesimally small though it is a critical feature of design for say high speed aircraft or Formula One racing cars; maybe sometimes one can know too much about a subject! Sometimes one reads of systems for producing changes, let us say for the line rating of a rod, where one is advised to simply add or subtract a certain amount (maybe 5 thou) at each station along the rod's length. Such advice however is not the best that can be offered if a rod of similar action is desired because 5 thou as a proportion of the tip will be greatly different from what it will be at the butt, though the new rod will be stronger or weaker as the case may be as it will contain more or less material than the original. 'Good' rod design is likely to mean different things to different people whose opinions will not be constrained by the mathematics or any other system which produce a 'notional' best design as personal preference and foibles will have much to do with it. For instance, I do not favour rods with excessively stiff butts, i.e. those that start to swell very markedly a couple of inches above the handgrip despite the fact that I realise that rods exhibiting this feature keep the propulsive force ahead of the hand and are highly esteemed by some fly fishers for cosmetic if for no other reasons. This dislike is not a purely irrational objection but is based on the idea that if a natural material is being used then the more one is able to spread the load along its length the better. For example, if one has say an 8'0" rod there is not much point in forcing about 7' (as mentioned on page 86) of it to do all the work which will pretty much be the case if the butt swells as some I have seen, making it, relative to the rest of the rod, as stiff as a poker and acting as a lever that might over stress the finer parts of the rod and may well cause plastic deformation (i.e. a permanent bend) particularly if there is a slightly weak point somewhere in the tip end. This does not mean of course that I want a rod that bends spinelessly right down through the handle though some element of give in this area does not discomfort me and should lead to a more durable rod and in theory at least should reduce the chances of the finer parts taking an unsightly set – in rather the same way as the dips cut on long bow limbs (see page 86) reduce their tendency to follow the string.

Something that has not been mentioned in the foregoing are stress curves which I do not trouble myself with in the sense that I plot the curves for each rod made which would anyway be the wrong time to undertake the calculation as any anomaly would then be part of the rod which is probably quite remiss of me. However in a practical way I do pay heed to the notion of avoiding sudden very marked reductions in diameter or rod tips that are hugely different from the butts, i.e. very thick butts matched with very fine tips, as such areas may well be subject to far more stress than is appropriate. This may in turn lead to the plastic deformation referred to above particularly if there is a weakness in the construction at some point. This may seem a simplistic approach to the subject but it has allowed me to make rods that have avoided taking the quite marked sets of some that I have seen and been asked to straighten. Two anglers favouring rods of very differing actions may cast equally well given comparable levels of skill and experience and catch equal numbers of fish. At some point they will have 'taken to' a rod with a particular action and become proficient with it, so maybe there is no such thing as a universally 'best' design for something as personal as a fly rod.

And finally a disclaimer (!) before some examples of the calculations are set out. What has been set down here are procedures that I have found informative and effective in generally producing the results that I have been seeking but not invariably at the first attempt though usually with such 'misses' the initial effort has been close enough as to require but little adjusting to ultimately produce that which was sought after. If you do get around to designing and making a rod you must take responsibility for the figures that you employ to make sure that they make sense in relation to what you wish to achieve.

Using the formula

To increase or decrease the line rating

Once a rod with a good/suitable action has been made then it is not difficult to calculate the increases or decreases in diameters to create a rod of similar action and length that will cast a heavier or lighter line.

The information required for this process is as follows:

1. The sizes/diameters of the original rod.
2. The original line size (weight).
3. The new line size (weight).
4. The relevant formula.

The example that follows illustrates the process using the Diary Rod dimensions as the starting point (original rod).

Rod sizes	Top section		Butt section	
(Original Ø s) at...	0"	0.078"	50"	0.225"
	5"	0.090"	55"	0.240"
	10"	0.107"	60"	0.255"
	15"	0.120"	65"	0.270"
	20"	0.135"	70"	0.285"
	25	0.150"	75"	0.290"
	30"	0.165"	80"	0.300"
	35"	0.180"	85"	0.310"
	40"	0.195"	90"	0.312"
	45"	0.210"	96"	0.315"

Line weights in grains for 10 yards of 'DT' lines

Line size	Weight	Line size	Weight
1	60	2	80
3	100	4	120
5	140	6	160
7	185	8	230
9	240	10	280
11	330	12	380

Let us suppose that we wish to increase the size of the above rod from a #5 line to a #6.

Using the formula wl^3/d^4 we need to discover what % increase in diameter will create a rod suitable for a #6 line. We can find out how much **w** will increase by referring to the line weight chart above – a #5 line weighs 140 grains and #6 line 160 which is an increase of 14%.

The next stage requires making a guess of how much **d** (diameter) will have to increase to make **w** (weight) 14% larger or put another way for it not to weigh 140 grains but 160 grains. Let us try 4% (not very much but a small increase in diameter will greatly affect a rod's stiffness).

l the length of the rod is to remain the same so in effect it can be forgotten about in the calculation, it is **d** and **w** that concern us and what happens to the one must happen to the other.

d is to increase by 4% (104% of its present value)

d^4 is 104% of 104% of 104% of 104% or $(1.14) = 116\%$

If **d** increases to 116% then so must **w** which was originally 140 grains

116% of 140 is 162 which is almost exactly the weight of a #6 line

Conclusion

The diameters of the #5 line rod will have to be increased by 4% to make the new #6 rod. If the guess had been too big or too small then an adjustment would have to have been made and the calculation done again.

The sizes for the 'new rod' are as follows:

Top section		Butt section	
0"	0.081"	50"	0.234"
5"	0.093"	55"	0.249"
10"	0.111"	60"	0.265"
15"	0.124"	65"	0.280"
20"	0.140"	70"	0.296"
25"	0.156"	75"	0.301"
30"	0.171"	80"	0.312"
35"	0.187"	85"	0.322"
40"	0.202"	90"	0.324"
45"	0.218"	96"	0.325"

In practice the tip diameter (0") and that at the 5" mark need not be increased and can remain the same as those for the #5 rod which are plenty strong enough for this new rod. A mathematically calculated tip dimension for a rod such as this would actually produce a diameter in the region of 50 thou which is too fine for practical use and in terms of ease of construction.

The table below makes unnecessary the whole business of going through the calculations each time a rod of the same length but a different weight of line is required – the data relates to 'trout sized' rods for use with line sizes from 3 through to 7.

Increase in line size		Increase in rod ø
From	**To**	
3	4	5%
4	5	4.5%
5	6	4%
6	7	3.5%

It is also useful to know that an increase in length of 10% will result in a reduction in loading of about 15% whereas a reduction in length of the same amount results in an increased loading of about 25%. From this data it is then possible to calculate the diameters for longer or shorter rods. In general I do not try to lengthen a rod in this fashion to any great extent but tend to keep alterations to no more than 6" which can usually be achieved with a reasonable expectation of producing a rod with the desired action. If a much longer rod is required – say an increase from 8'0" to 9'0" – then probably it is preferable to start the design process again, though I am sure there are those who successfully achieve this degree of 'lengthening' without doing so.

Epilogue

In conclusion – some bits and pieces

All sorts of questions can arise when a rod is completed, some of which will be of a technical nature relating to its action, performance, longevity, etc. that only use and time will answer: other questions of the 'daydreaming' type may also come to mind. Will this rod play its part in the landing of a 'truly no need to lie' specimen falls into this latter category which is the sort of query that can set the imagination running in a quite unrealistic way when the season is still months away or even in full swing. Nevertheless a new rod always causes a flutter of hope which is supposed to spring eternal – particularly, maybe, in respect of fishermen and rod makers. However despite the wishful thinking that is only occasionally mirrored in reality the 'bank balance' of pleasures involved in the process of rod making generally and in the making of a specific rod far outweigh the tribulations of which there always seem to be some (which are best forgotten!) so it might be a good idea to round off this account with some of the things that appear on the credit side of the balance, some of which have been touched on in the foregoing text.

The principal 'good thing' must be that the whole business of rod making and then fishing with the results of the hours spent in the workshop and of hearing of the exploits of friends using their rods remains enjoyable. Some of the rods, given to those friends and fellow fly fishers, have travelled far farther than their maker. One reached the Falkland Islands in the days before that place was drawn to everyone's attention for reasons less pleasant than the fishing which by all accounts is excellent; others were used in New Zealand where their qualities were tested to the limit judging by the photographs I received, one of which had written on the back 'Just look at the bend!', words guaranteed to make me apprehensive as it was rather too impressive a bend. I suspect that those kiwi rods had short, very exciting lives being used to subdue fish of a size for which they were not really designed. Rods however do not have to be used in distant parts to cause a bit of excitement and some of the best moments have been watching friends catch more modest fish on local waters. However as this booklet has been concerned primarily with the practicalities of making a rod I will pick out some of the practical aspects of the craft that have also left good memories.

Whilst it is important to learn all you can from the experience of others great fun can be had if you avoid regarding such knowledge as being set in stone and thus never to be questioned and approach the enterprise in a curious and imaginative way. It is of course inevitable that the great majority of what one will undertake will be what has been set down by others but it is also probably true that what one learns from one's individual efforts will have a special place in the body of knowledge accumulated. I have especially enjoyed those many times fiddling about in the workshop when trying to devise a simpler way of achieving a certain end or by sometimes using knowledge gained in a different craft and applying it to the problem in hand or simply trying out an idea that seemed to go against the general grain of thinking. I use the term 'fiddling about' advisedly as a result of having been tracked down to the workshop one day by one of my grandchildren who promptly announced 'Ah, this is where you come to fiddle about', words that had to be paid heed to as she holds world class status in the subject – out of the mouths of babes and sucklings, etc. etc... I always thought I was experimenting or even indulging in some R&D; so we are brought to earth!

Some of the ideas that emerged from this experimenting, correction (!), fiddling about, include the following:

The use of 'paper build-up' runners to control the taper of grooves for both the preparation and finishing of splines at a time before the more usual methods employed today became widely known; the rough knife-triangulation of the bamboo strips prior to making them into splines and the use of the L shaped tempering frame, all quite simple personal ideas that worked when they were first thought of and are still in use today to some degree. The use of a multi-stranded knotted driving belt devised for the Garrison type spline binder questioned the conventional wisdom that suggests that a knot in a belt will jam things up. Some fiddling about demonstrated that in reality such a belt will work splendidly, in addition to which it is so much easier to make than its spliced counterpart that it encourages one to make and keep handy a number of spares. The addition of 'wings' on either side of the device to support the rod section before, during and after binding was also a very useful idea.

The spliced joint rods described opened up a new area of inquiry and interest at a time when conventional rods had been made for many years and the question of how many ought to be accumulated was becoming very valid, and though I had no intention of ceasing to make conventional rods this different type freshened my interest in both the craft and at the riverside. The use of masking tape as the securing medium, although intended as an interim method, also proved to be an enduringly good solution. Rods of this type have also offered my companions the opportunity to use items not usually (at all?) available in the normal course of things which gave them direct and me vicarious pleasure. Of course none of these things are important in the great scheme of things and will not set the rod making world alight though they illustrated that certain procedures could be simplified without compromising the quality of the end product and a resurrected idea could be of practical use which was satisfying at a personal level.

One aspect of the enjoyment that can be derived from this or any other pastime that I have neglected badly involves contact with other rod makers, of whom I have met very few. Such neglect is in general not very wise (even if one has a tendency to follow one's own path) as interaction even at a distance with other like-minded people both in terms of camaraderie and exchange of knowledge is very valuable and is likely to hasten your progress considerably. Maybe what we were told as children holds good here – 'Don't do as I do, do as I say!'

So there you have it. I hope you have found it enjoyable and maybe useful even if you do not wish to make a rod. If what has been set out does act as a catalyst and you make a rod and catch a few fish with it I will certainly deem the exercise to have been worthwhile.

Good luck!

'Just look at the bend!'

Sources of information and bibliography

The Internet makes available a huge amount of information about split bamboo rods in general and some that is aimed specifically at rod makers. A search engine such as Google or Yahoo will offer pages and pages of information and if a little time is spent sifting through them the relevant data will be identified, some of which will be offered by individuals, some by rod making groups and yet more by firms. Most of the information seems to be generated in the USA where there are surely many more people involved in the pursuit than in the UK.

Indeed it would not be exaggerating to write that the Internet could be the source of all the information you require, including direct contact with other rod makers.

Just as the Internet may be regarded as the starting point for a wide range of information, all sorts of specialist bookshops and publishers are a good place to start if one wishes to build up a collection of relevant books – if you get on to their mailing lists you be constantly appraised of new publications. The specialist nature and relatively small demand for such books makes them little seen in general outlets and many were published years ago and are not easily sourced without specialist help, though contact with your library service may well help in this respect – it certainly did in years gone by. Sometimes books that concern split bamboo rods but are not technical in content can be used as a source of such information. For example, Gierach's *Fishing Bamboo* (Lyons Press) which falls into this category has a bibliography that lists a number of titles that are relevant to rod makers in addition to those whose interest is in say the historical aspects of the subject.

Coch y Bondu
Booksellers and publishers specialising in fishing books who offer a very wide range of books including those of a technical nature. www.anglebooks.com

Alder Creek Enterprises, Inc
Publishers of books and pamphlets on split bamboo rod making.

The Planing Form
A newsletter wholly concerned with split bamboo rod making and two books called *Best of the Planing Form (Vols. 1 & 2)* that can be sourced at aldercreek@core.com

The Angler's Bamboo by Luis Marden (Lyons and Burford)
A book describing Tonkin cane rather than rod building per se but very useful for background information.

A Master's Guide to Building a Bamboo Fly Rod by Garrison and Carmichael (Meadow Run Press)
Gives exhaustive details for building a rod and if just one book is to be purchased on the subject then probably it is this one.

Rod Building for Amateurs by Richard Walker (an Angling Times publication).

How to Build your own Split Cane Fishing Rod by Col. Lawton Moss (Technical Press Ltd).

I include these last two books which were first published decades ago because they were titles I found useful when I started rod making (also decades ago!)